D1204264

LEE

OF

VIRGINIA

By DOUGLAS SOUTHALL FREEMAN

LEE OF VIRGINIA

GEORGE WASHINGTON, VOLUMES I–VI
VOLUME VII, *by J. A. Carroll and Mary W. Ashworth completes the biography.*

LEE'S LIEUTENANTS, VOLUMES I–III

R. E. LEE, VOLUMES I–IV

THE SOUTH TO POSTERITY

39229

THE LIBRARY
du PONT MANUAL HIGH SCHOOL
LOUISVILLE, KENTUCKY

LEE
OF
VIRGINIA

DOUGLAS SOUTHALL FREEMAN

CHARLES SCRIBNER'S SONS   NEW YORK

© 1958 Estate of Douglas Southall Freeman

This book published simultaneously in the United States of America and in Canada.
Copyright under the Berne Convention.

All rights reserved.
No part of this book may be reproduced in any form
without the permission of Charles Scribner's Sons.

E–4.61[V]

PRINTED IN THE UNITED STATES OF AMERICA

LIBRARY OF CONGRESS CATALOG CARD NUMBER 58-11643

PUBLISHER'S PREFACE

In 1944, Douglas Southall Freeman, with the four volumes of his Pulitzer-Prize biography of R. E. Lee to his credit, had just completed his three-volume history-biography of Lee's Lieutenants. He was not yet willing, however, to leave the great figures of the Confederacy. By way of relaxation before starting on the massive *George Washington* which was to occupy his remaining years, he wrote a one-volume biography of Robert E. Lee. This was a project close to his heart, for he had wanted especially to present the revered Southern leader to those for whom the reading of the four-volume definitive work would seem too large an undertaking. Although he began the work in response to a suggestion that he write a biography for a somewhat younger age-level, the public he always had wanted most to reach with Lee's story was that of the young adults, and it was only natural that the resulting biography should shape itself as a book for them.

Judging the book too mature in treatment to serve its original purpose, Freeman laid it aside. Once absorbed in the research and writing of his multiple-volume life of George Washington, he put all other projects out of his mind. When sudden death came to him in 1953 the manuscript of this one-volume biography of Lee was still among his papers. It was complete, however, and had received his usual careful revision. We are publishing it now in the hope that it will provide a whole generation with an inspiring portrait of a great and beloved American.

Contents

List of Illustrations

LEE

OF

VIRGINIA

CHAPTER ONE

A Backward Glance

R OBERT LEE was like every other boy: he was not quite certain when memory began. In the dim zone of his earliest childhood, he confused what he had done with what he had been told he had done. His clearest mental picture was of a great house with a vast central hallway and a tremendous attic. In the eastern wing of the house, overlooking the flower garden, was the sunny room in which his mother told him he had been born on the 19th of January, 1807. In front of the house, as he remembered it, was a lawn of "several hundred acres, adorned with cedars, oaks and forest poplars." Stratford the place was called, and in Robert's young eyes it was a wonderland of beauty.

Perhaps the brown-eyed, black-haired boy was lucky in not remembering more at that time about the Lee plantation on the Potomac River in Westmoreland County, Virginia. It had fame but it had sorrow, too. Inside the doors hung chains. If Robert ever saw them, he did not understand that they had been put there to keep out officers of the law who came to collect bills that Robert's father could not pay. For ten months, about the time Robert was beginning to talk, his father was never at home. If the little boy asked where his father was, he was told only that his father had gone away but was coming back. Truth was, his father was in jail, not because of any crime but because of debt.

It was a sad, sad story. Robert's father was Henry Lee, who had been the leader of mounted soldiers known in the American Revolutionary War as "Lee's Legion." He himself was sometimes called Colonel Lee and sometimes General Lee, but he was known to old soldiers as "Light Horse Harry" Lee, because the arms and equipment of his troops were "light." General Washington had been proud of "Light Horse Harry." After the war, the Virginia Legislature had elected Lee Governor three times in succession. Henry Lee then had served in Congress and at the observance of Washington's death had made a speech in which he had used words which most Americans remember. Washington, said Lee, was "first in war, first in peace, and first in the hearts of his countrymen."

Lee was brilliant, charming in his conversation and devoted to his family, but he could not resist the temptation to speculate. As he did not possess good business judgment, he lost everything he had. That was why he was put in prison under the curious old law which provided that a man could be locked up where he could not possibly earn money to pay his debts.

When "Light Horse Harry" at last was released from prison in 1810, he and his family faced new trouble. Henry Lee had been married twice. His first wife, who was his cousin, had owned Stratford and, at his death, had left it to her son who also was named Henry. This younger Henry, born in 1787, had become 21 in 1808 when Robert was a baby. Stratford then became lawfully his and should be turned over to him. This meant that Henry Lee and his wife must provide a new home for their children who then numbered four. Charles Carter, the oldest, was nearly 12; Ann was 10; Sydney Smith, usually called Smith, was 8. All three of these needed schooling. Robert would, also, in a few years. The most suitable place that had good schools was the town of Alexandria, about eighty miles up the

winding Potomac. At Alexandria, Henry Lee would be among kinspeople and would be close to the city of Washington.

The family moved to Alexandria in the summer of 1810 but the
tragedy of "Light Horse Harry" did not end there. Another war with
Great Britain was in prospect. Henry Lee opposed this war and, in
doing so, gave his support to a young editor in Baltimore, Maryland,
who was writing against American entry into the war. One day in
1812, when Henry Lee was in Baltimore, a crowd of mad, drunken
men tried to wreck the printing-office of the paper. In the fighting, Lee
was badly beaten and was left for dead. He survived and finally
reached home but he never recovered fully. In 1813 he went to the
British West Indies to recover his health and there he remained for
five years. On his way home, in 1818, "Light Horse Harry" died on
Cumberland Island, Georgia. In some ways he had made a failure of
his life, but Mrs. Lee always spoke of him in terms of love and respect
and taught her children to do so. In Robert's eyes, his father always
was a hero of the Revolutionary War, the young companion of Washington.

Washington himself was a living influence, if not a living person, in
the city of Alexandria, where the Lees continued to reside after the
death of "Light Horse Harry." The church attended by Mrs. Lee and
the children was the one in which Washington had worshipped. Hundreds of persons who lived in Alexandria during Robert's youth remembered Washington and would describe his appearance and his
manner when he came to the city from his home down the Potomac
at Mt. Vernon. Some boys might have tired of all this talk about
Washington, but Robert did not. Washington was the hero of his
hero, who was his father, and therefore Washington was Robert's hero,
too.

The town was interesting to boys for much besides the memorials of Washington. Outside Alexandria were wide, marshy fields, known as King George's Meadows, where every sort of adventure might be had. The docks were fascinating. Foreign ships often were anchored there. Sailors who spoke strange languages came ashore in outlandish clothing. In quiet coves along the clear river, there was perfect swimming. Often in winter there were long stretches of ice that would support all the skaters of Alexandria.

There was one place even more interesting to Robert than Alexandria or Stratford. That place was Shirley, his mother's old home on James River. It was a long way from Alexandria, whether you went by vessel or by carriage, but when a boy got there, he had no end of delight. Mrs. Lee, before her marriage, had been Ann Carter, daughter of Charles Carter. He had been probably the wealthiest man of his time in Virginia, and had lived in great style, and with abounding charity to all those in distress. Twenty-five thousand acres of land and hundreds of slaves were his. By his two marriages he had no less than twenty-three children, but when he died in 1806, he had sufficient property to provide for all those of his blood who had survived infancy. It was from the income of a trust fund left by him that Mrs. Lee had been able to live in moderate comfort after "Light Horse Harry" had lost everything.

Shirley remained in the family and always had open doors for Ann Lee and her children. The fine old house was crowded with portraits and beautiful furniture. A hanging staircase was the admiration of all visitors. Opposite one entrance were the flower gardens. From porch and windows one might look across the muddy but friendly James. The plantation was rich in crops of every sort but it was much more than a farm. To care for all who lived there—free and slave, workers and aged and children—the place had to be self-sustaining. Sugar, coffee, spices and some clothing and machinery had to be purchased, of course. Almost everything else was grown or manufactured "on the place." The slaves were divided into three groups, the house servants, the mechanics and the field hands. Many of the house servants had fine manners and had adopted the viewpoint of their masters. Often the mechanics, developing skill, would buy their own freedom. The field hands or farm laborers were those who had the hardest life and the least chance of advancement.

Robert came to know all this about Shirley. If he had been a girl, he would have known Shirley even better, because he would have gone to school there. The Carters were so numerous that they maintained two schools for their children. Besides the one at Shirley for girls, there was one for boys at Eastern View, Fauquier County, the home of one of Mrs. Lee's sisters, Elizabeth Carter Randolph.

To this school Robert went about 1816. It was in reality a friendly home, not a school, but it did not have quite the discipline Robert had known at home. When he came back to Alexandria after his first stay at Eastern View, his mother thought he was getting self-willed and in writing Mrs. Randolph her thanks for the kind treatment of the boy, she remarked that Robert was difficult to handle. Mrs. Randolph replied that she had found Robert "a most engaging child." If he was getting out of hand, the only advice she could give Mrs. Lee was that which she had applied to her own sons, which was "to whip and pray, and pray and whip." Actually, Robert needed little whipping. He was a strong, handsome, healthy boy who loved to have his fun, but he learned early that he had duties to perform. If they had to be done, they were more easily and more quickly done if he kept his temper than if he lost it.

When Robert had received all the instruction offered at Eastern View, he came back home and entered the Alexandria Academy, which was an excellent school. Besides study, Robert found time for sports

—riding, hunting, swimming—and for a nearer, dearer duty, which was that of helping to care for his mother. She was failing fast in health and sometimes scarcely could leave her room. Carter could not help her, because he was at Harvard, where he was studying law. Smith had entered the navy as a midshipman; Ann was sickly and often had to stay in Philadelphia to get medical attention. The fifth child, Mildred, who had been born after the family came to Alexandria, was too young to be of much help. Robert was of just the age and temperament to wait on his mother and to "run the house." With his mother, he talked often of what he should do in life, and after he completed his course at the Alexandria Academy, he went to work on his plans. His half-brother Henry helped him loyally. So did several Congressmen who remembered "Light Horse Harry" with affection. How much of a secret the family made of the plans, it is impossible to say now. If there was a secret, it came out one day in March, 1824, when an official paper was brought Robert from the post office.

CHAPTER TWO

How to Get Ahead at West Point

ROBERT COULD ENTER West Point and begin training as a soldier. That was the great news the letter brought. President James Monroe had named him a cadet at the United States Military Academy. John C. Calhoun, Secretary of War, wrote to tell Robert of the appointment the boy had been trying for months to procure. The only thing to dampen the family's rejoicing was the fact that many young men were ahead of Robert on the list. He could not be admitted until July, 1825—a year and three months in the future.

That seemed a long time to wait but it turned out to Robert's advantage in this way: During the autumn of 1824, a young Quaker named Benjamin Hallowell came to Alexandria and opened a school in which he offered instruction higher than that given at the Alexandria Academy. In February, 1825, after the new teacher had shown that he knew his business, Robert enrolled with him in order to "freshen up" on mathematics and to get a "running start" on the work at West Point. Robert liked his teacher and found later that his whole career was aided by those three months at the Quaker's school. Mr. Hallowell was equally impressed by Robert, about whom he later wrote these interesting words: "His specialty was *finishing up*. He imparted a finish and a neatness, as he proceeded, to everything he undertook. One of the branches of mathematics he studied with me was Conic Sections, in which some of the diagrams were very complicated. He drew the diagrams on a slate; and although he well knew that the one he was drawing would have to be removed to make room for another, he drew each one with as much accuracy and finish, lettering and all, as if it were to be engraved and printed."

When Robert reached West Point during the last week of June, 1825, he found that the neatness he had learned at home and had displayed at Mr. Hallowell's was one of the qualities required of every cadet. Diligence was another. Good conduct was a third. Patience was a fourth and was demanded particularly of newcomers. No cadet was admitted until formally examined and approved, and even after that had been done, he was on probation for six months. If he failed at any time from stupidity or laziness or lack of discipline, out he went!

Robert was accepted on the 28th and was assigned a place in a tent on "the plain," as the parade and camp ground was styled. Doubtless Robert wrote home promptly and often, but as none of his letters survives, it is impossible to say what his first impressions of West Point were or whether he became homesick. He found the buildings of the Military Academy to be few and crude. The food was notoriously bad. Life was stern and simple, but the glory of the site and the beauty of the Hudson River were inspiring then and always afterward to Robert, who had a deep love of Nature.

For the first two months, while the cadet corps was under canvas, no classes were held. Four hours of drill and the work of keeping their camp clean were the day's routine. Before the end of August, the cadets returned to barracks where they lived three or four in a room on a schedule that had to be observed to the last bugle-call. At daybreak, the men arose, dressed, answered roll-call and had half-an-hour for cleaning their arms and their rooms or "quarters." After their rooms had been inspected, the men worked over their books until 7 o'clock.

Then came breakfast, and then four hours of mathematics—three in class and one of individual review. At noon the fourth-classmen or "plebes" turned to their only other study, which was French, and, after dinner at 1 P.M., they had freedom until 2 o'clock. French then demanded two hours of classroom time. Two more of drill made the cadets ready for supper at sundown. When the meal was over, they studied till 9:30. Lights went out at 10. In cold weather, the rooms scarcely were warm enough for the men to use their hands without discomfort. Sickness in winter was general and sometimes severe. To endure the life for four years was an achievement; to win good marks and to keep out of trouble was a triumph.

No matter how hard the daily life, Robert resolved to excel without being a hermit. He liked people and he quickly made friends. A classmate named Jack Mackay, who came from Georgia, and a fellow-Virginian, Joseph E. Johnston, commonly called "The Colonel," were among those to whom Robert quickly became attached. Outside his own class he looked with awe on the magnificent adjutant of the cadet corps, Albert Sidney Johnston, and he no doubt admired, also, a tall, thin Mississippian, Jefferson Davis. A few weeks in class showed Robert who were the ablest men in his class of eighty-seven. Those with whom he had to match wits were Charles Mason, a New Yorker, an Ohio cadet named Catharinus Buckingham, a Georgian named William Harford, and perhaps one or two others whose abilities were not quite so plain as those of this brilliant trio. If Robert was to keep up with them, or was to get ahead of them, he had to plan his work and his play so that he could make the most of every minute. He had to avoid demerits, too! There was no short cut to the top of the class: It was work, work, work—every weekday.

Robert kept his back straight on parade ground, but he bent his neck over his books. Night after night, morning after morning, he studied his mathematics and his French. He had not had any French before he came to West Point and he found the idioms and the irregular verbs difficult. They simply had to be learned—that was all there was to it. For this task he had one advantage besides a good mind: He was strong enough in character to resist the temptation to slip away at night and go to North's Tavern. In violation of rules, many of the cadets went to that "out-of-bounds" resort and spent their money and their hours, though they often were caught and punished. Colonel Sylvanus Thayer, the Superintendent of the Academy, was supposed to have spies who reported these delinquents. The commandant of cadets, Major William Worth, was known to walk around the grounds at night and to haunt the barracks at the oddest hours. That was why his nickname was "Old Hant." Robert had no trouble with "Old Hant," and by staying away from North's he got ahead of many boys who went there; but so did most of the cadets Robert had to outstrip if he was to be a leader in his class. They did not "take a chance." Their hours were as strict and their attention to drill as precise as Robert's.

The first showing of "who was where" came after the first half-year's examinations, which were held in January, 1826. Robert did well but he had comrades who did equally well. He was tied with Buckingham, Harford and Mason in mathematics, and as the "L" of his name put him alphabetically third, he got that place on the record. In French he was fifth. His conduct rating was without a demerit, though here, again, probably because of the alphabet, he stood No. 3. He was "off probation," of course, and was headed, evidently, for a fine race with the other leaders of his class.

At the end of another six months, he found that he had not gained. He was fourth in mathematics and fifth in French and he still had a clean conduct sheet. In "general merit" he was No. 3. Mason was first; Harford second. This standing did not satisfy Robert, but it made him a "distinguished cadet" and assured the publication of his name in the next edition of the *Army Register*. His highest reward for a year of honest attention to all his duties was appointment as staff sergeant. This was an unusual honor for a man just ending his first year and passing from the fourth class to the third. Robert had won it by diligence, by fine bearing, by good conduct and by a realization that a cadet had to be "good" in everything, and not merely in the subject of his special interest.

During the summer encampment of 1826, Robert had his first artillery drill. When the autumn came, Staff Sergeant Lee and his classmates had another and a less pleasant novelty: They began to study drawing, about which most of them knew nothing. Fortunately their teacher, Thomas Gimbrède, a Frenchman, had ingenuity and a sense of humor. He eased the anxiety of the cadets by demonstrating logically that any person could draw. There were, he said, only two lines in drawing, a straight line and a curved line. Anybody could draw a straight line; anybody could draw a curved line. Therefore, any one could draw.

The boys may have questioned his logic but they had to take his course. Robert had drawn many straight lines on his slate at Mr. Hallowell's school and he had drawn some curved lines in preparing his diagrams. He had no special skill in combining straight lines and curves but he gave to drawing the same attention and the same hard work he displayed in his mathematics and his French. It perhaps was during his first study of drawing that he made this discovery, which he often applied later in the bloody contention of war: The attainment of success does not always call for perfection. Success may consist, sometimes, of making fewer mistakes than the other fellow does. If Robert could avoid bad mistakes in drawing, even though he developed no great skill, he still might keep in the top group.

In this reasoning he was to prove himself correct. He may not have been equally wise in accepting part time employment that winter as Acting Assistant Professor of Mathematics at $10 a month. The post was an honor; the money was welcome; but there was a danger that the work would take time Robert needed for his own studies. At first, he was so well up in his studies that he could stand the added strain. After the examinations of January, 1827, he stood fourth in mathematics, fifth in French and fifth in drawing; in conduct he was without demerit. This was fine but it still was not quite enough. Robert went to work more vigorously than ever with a determination to win the furlough that cadets of good standing received at the close of their second year. When the grades for the spring term were posted and the year's standing was determined, in June, 1827, Robert still had fourth place in mathematics, but he had climbed from fifth to fourth in drawing. He remained fifth in French. His conduct and his drill record helped him this time, because they had been sustained for two years. He was listed as No. 2 in general merit and was above Harford. Only Charles Mason was ahead of Robert.

The vacation of two months Robert spent in Virginia. It was a happy season except for one thing: The condition of Mrs. Lee was far worse than when Robert had left her in 1825. Robert spent much of his vacation in her company, and when he went to visit some of his kinspeople, he took her with him. He always was grateful afterward that he had that further opportunity of listening to her wise, gentle words.

In what she and his friends did and said, Robert was happily absorbed and never was self-conscious. He did not realize he was making a new impression on his circle. Already, at the Academy, the boys were calling him the "Marble Model." If a certain sharp-chinned, attractive girl in a great house on a hill above Alexandria saw Robert that summer, she probably approved that nickname. Probably, too, she did not turn her head away when he looked at her and smiled. When he had gone to West Point, he had been a fine-looking boy. His friends agreed, on his return, that he had become a handsome young man. About five feet, eleven inches in height, he had ruddy skin, black hair with a touch of curl in it, flawless white teeth, and eyes that were a dark brown, though indoors they looked black. One of his fellow-cadets wrote of him: "Though firm in his position and perfectly erect, he had none of the stiffness so often assumed by men who affect to be very strict in their ideas of what is military."

Back at the Academy in the autumn of 1827, when something in the air conveyed warning that winter was stirring already up the Hudson, Robert found new attraction in new studies. There was no more theoretical mathematics and no more French. In their place were physics and chemistry and some additional time for drawing. By giving to this routine his fullest energy, Robert was able to discharge his duties as an assistant in mathematics and also to keep the pace of his fast-moving competitors. He was, if possible, more diligent than ever because he had another prize in mind: At the end of this third year, the most coveted honor of the cadet corp was to be awarded. One or another of the men who combined fine class-standing with high distinction in drill would be named corps adjutant. That cadet officer formed the battalion for dress parade and other ceremonies and commanded it until he turned it over to the Commandant of Cadets. Robert was ambitious to have that post and was willing to work for it.

The January examinations showed Robert second in physics, third in chemistry and fourth in drawing. By June, he had pulled up to third place in drawing and he had held his second place in physics and his third in chemistry. As there was not one black mark on his conduct or drill record, he was again No. 2—and corps adjutant!

His friends were proud of him. Said "Joe" Johnston many years later: ". . . no other youth or man so united the qualities that win warm friendship and command high respect. For he was full of sympathy and kindness, genial and fond of gay conversation, and even of fun, while his correctness of demeanor and attention to all duties, personal and official, and a dignity as much a part of himself as the elegance of his person, gave him a superiority that everyone acknowledged in his heart."

The last year at West Point, which opened with this shining honor of cadet adjutancy, was the most absorbing of them all for Robert. Drawing was dropped. So was physics, though chemistry was continued. A course on rhetoric and moral philosophy was given, but the emphasis of the year was on a subject that Robert soon came to love above them all—engineering and the science of war. To master this combined course, while instructing in mathematics and acting as corps adjutant, Robert had to work to the absolute limit, and had to use his ingenuity and his best judgment in finding extra hours. Because of some unexplained difficulty, he felt that he should get coaching in geology during the late autumn. With the help of this and of regular, concentrated study, he made a splendid showing in the January examinations: He was second in chemistry and geology, was second in moral philosophy, and was tied with Buckingham at the head of the class in engineering. For the first time in any subject, this rating put him ahead of Charles Mason. Encouraged by this, Robert prepared for the final spurt on the home stretch, the concluding term of the entire four years. Late in April, as the final examinations approached, he got temporary relief as adjutant and procured from the Superintendent permission to board at the hotel, so that he could save time for his studies.

At last the special board of visitors arrived and put each cadet through five separate oral examinations of one hour each. During these examinations any one of the visitors could ask the cadet any question on any subject studied during the year. Robert kept his head through-out this grilling and emerged as top man in artillery and tactics. His conduct record was clean to the last hour. In general merit, he was No. 2—next to Charles Mason. This standing gave Robert the privilege of selecting the branch or "arm" of the service in which he would be commissioned as an officer. He chose engineering, which he had found fascinating. After the simple commencement he received his diploma, drew the $103 he had saved from his pay and allowances, and went home on a two months' furlough as Brevet Second Lieuten-ant Robert Edward Lee, Corps of Engineers, United States Army. He saw little after that of the men who had been his rivals at West Point. Charles Mason remained two years as Principal Assistant Professor of Engineering and then resigned to become a lawyer. William Harford served in the infantry for four years and left the service for private engineer work, but he died before he was 30. Catharinus Bucking-ham, who slipped to sixth place in his last year, had a fine, long career as engineer, teacher, merchant, soldier and author of books on mathematics.

CHAPTER THREE

Training for an Opportunity

THE SUMMER MONTHS at home during Robert's furlough of 1829 should have been among the happiest of his life. They were, in one sense, because he became more and more interested in that sharp-chinned girl in the big house up the Potomac. In a different sense, the time was one of the saddest of Lee's life. When he arrived home, he found his mother extremely ill. On the 10th of July, she died.

This loss of his mother was one from which Robert never recovered altogether. Late in his life, when he had a thousand memories of great deeds of battle, he remembered every detail of her passing and he said often that he "owed everything to her." Although he kept her shrine in his grateful heart, he wrote scarcely anything about her. Their letters disappeared long ago. Little consequently is known of her. Dimly one sees a woman of wisdom and of faith who had profound concern for the welfare of her children. The other characteristics of Ann Carter Lee are hidden in the impenetrable shadows of time.

Before Robert's first grief was past, he received from the Chief of Engineers orders to report to Cockspur Island in the Savannah River, Georgia. This assignment meant that Lieutenant Lee would be pleasantly close to the gracious city of Savannah, where his friend Jack Mackay lived. There was advantage in the post, also, for this reason: On the death of his mother, Robert became responsible for Nat, the oldest of the few Negro slaves Mrs. Lee owned. This faithful man was regarded as a member of the family, and as he was in frail health, there was a chance that the warm winter climate of the Georgia coast might benefit him.

When Robert arrived at Cockspur Island with Nat, he found that these two advantages were about all that could be said in behalf of his station. Everything else was adverse. The task of the engineers was to construct a strong fort on a swampy island where foundations might prove unstable. As this large project was in the first stage, Robert had to spend many hours in water and mud up to his arm pits while he made the necessary surveys for canals to drain the swamp. Then, too, Nat's health grew worse instead of better until the old man became helpless and before many months passed away. The chief recompense for privation and loneliness on the island was the kindness of the Mackays. They were a fine, sociable family that included, among other members, a charming girl named Eliza. With her, Robert carried on a lively correspondence. He probably would have fallen in love with her if the memory of the girl in the great mansion up the river from Alexandria had not been so persistent and vivid.

Another compensation for months of solitude on the Savannah River was a brief opportunity of managing the entire project early in 1831, while the regular engineer was sick. The responsibility was great for a young man just 24, but it was brief. When the new supervisor of the work arrived and decided to change the plan of the fort on Cockspur Island, all work on the old design was stopped. As this left Robert with nothing to do, he was transferred to Fortress Monroe, on the northern side of Hampton Roads, Virginia.

This was a fine appointment. It placed Robert under an able and congenial officer, Capt. Andrew Talcott. Besides, Fortress Monroe was only one day's run by steamboat from home and kin and the girl in the mansion on the Potomac. During the one visit Robert had made to Alexandria, while stationed at Cockspur Island, he had seen her often. Now that he was near her again, he realized how much he loved her. She was named Mary Anne Randolph Custis and was the daughter of Mr. and Mrs. George Washington Parke Custis. He was the grandson of Mrs. George Washington and the adopted son of "the Father of the country," and he had spent most of his boyhood at Mt. Vernon.

In 1804, when he was 23, Custis had married Mary Lee Fitzhugh and had built a new home, styled Arlington, on the crest of a hill on the Virginia side of the Potomac River, opposite Washington. The mansion was conspicuous for its large portico and heavy columns, though its interior was not particularly attractive, except when the presence of Mary lighted its halls. She was the only surviving child of Mr. and Mrs. Custis and, of course, was some day to inherit Arlington, its plantation and the other large properties of the family.

It was not her wealth but herself that interested Robert. That sharp chin of hers was a little too long for beauty. Her nose, too, was more prominent than she would have liked it to be; but her abundant hair was pretty, and her eyes and her smile had a sparkle. She was vivacious and interested in people, a girl as popular with her own sex as she was with young men. She was 23—one year younger than Robert. He probably had known her since childhood and now that he was at Fortress Monroe, he came up the Potomac to visit her whenever he could. Mrs. Custis, who was kin to Robert, always was glad to see him, but Mr. Custis, though flawlessly polite, was not encouraging. Mary's father had nothing against Robert personally. Mr. Custis's lack of enthusiasm for the soldierly young guest must have been due to his knowledge that Robert had little besides army pay. Although Mr. Custis never said so, it is probable that he wanted Mary to marry some man with a fortune to match hers.

Photo by U. S. War Department, Washington, D. C.

ROBERT E. LEE

IN THE DRESS UNIFORM OF A LIEUTENANT OF ENGINEERS

Painted about 1838 by William E. West.

REPRODUCED THROUGH THE COURTESY OF THE PRESENT OWNER, MRS. RICHARD E. LEE, III

Robert had different plans. One day at Arlington, he was reading aloud to Mrs. Custis and to Mary from a new novel by Sir Walter Scott. The story proved so interesting that all three of them forgot the passage of time until Mrs. Custis thoughtfully interrupted the reading to say that Robert must be tired and hungry. Mary should get him some refreshment, perhaps some of the fruitcake on the sideboard, if he cared for it. The two went into the dining room together. When they came out, they were engaged. Mrs. Custis probably was pleased. Her husband did not raise any objection. As both Robert and Mary were old enough to know their own minds, nothing was to be gained by delay. The Lieutenant succeeded in getting a furlough from his duties at Fortress Monroe; Mary set June 30, 1831, as the date for the marriage.

It was the gayest affair, probably, that Arlington ever witnessed. Mary could not have less than six bridesmaids without offending one or another of her dearest friends. Robert brought a like number of groomsmen. All twelve of these guests were crowded into Arlington, where Mary's trousseau was immensely admired. One of her lovely gowns, the so-called "second-day dress," still attracts the eyes of visitors to the Valentine Museum, Richmond, where it is on display. The wedding dress itself contrasted beautifully with Robert's uniform.

All the arrangements seemed to be perfect until the very day of the wedding. Then there came a heavy rain. This was escaped by most of the guests, but not by the officiating minister, Rev. Reuel Keith. Caught by the storming while riding on horseback, he arrived at Arlington in wet garments and without any other suit to which he could change. All the groomsmen were officers who had with them only their uniforms. Mr. Custis had abundant apparel at hand, but he was short and fat, and Mr. Keith was tall and thin. There was no alternative to dropping the minister into coat and trousers of the bride's father. Mr. Keith looked ludicrous in this clothing, but, happily, he was able to conceal it under his cassock.

When the ceremony began, Mary was nervous and a bit scared. Robert was not quite as frightened as he expected he would be. In a vague way he felt as he had when called to the blackboard at West Point to demonstrate a difficult problem in mathematics. The minister, Robert wrote afterward, "had a few words to say, though he dwelt upon them as if he had been reading my death warrant, and there was a tremulousness in the hand I held that made me anxious for him to end."

There was a happy, month-long honeymoon. Then in August, 1831, the young couple went to live in the officers' quarters at Fortress Monroe, where Mary was welcomed for her own sake and as the wife of one of the most popular men at the station. Robert was then in his 25th year and had already on his countenance the marks of high thought and the promise of noble achievement. A cousin who saw him that autumn wrote later: "My eye fell upon his face in perfect repose, and the thought at once flashed through my mind: 'You certainly look more like a great man than anyone I have ever seen.'"

At the time, there did not appear to be any prospect of early attainment of anything great in Robert's profession. For six years, his duties were those of a junior construction engineer at Fortress Monroe (May, 1831–November, 1834), and those of an office assistant in Washington (November, 1834–April, 1837). The only other special task assigned him in this period was that of aiding during the summer of 1815 in the establishment of the disputed boundary-line between Michigan and Ohio.

Most of the work of these years was plain, dull routine, but it taught Lee that he had a certain measure of uninviting, unexciting duty to perform in the world, and that he did it most easily when he did it with the least complaint. A second gain was in learning more and more of the art of getting on with persons of every different type. From the humblest laborer to the Chief of the Corps of Engineers, he dealt with them and won their respect. Lee had an excellent sense of humor and teased the young women and bantered his male friends. He knew how to give and take but he refrained from joking about his friends in such a personal way that he prompted them to the same sort of jest. He was a part of every company at the same time that he refrained from being familiar.

After nine years of professional training and friendly relations, Robert Lee was qualified to make small opportunity large. In April, 1837, he was assigned to engineering duty on the Mississippi River at St. Louis with two projects in his care. One was that of clearing the Des Moines Rapids of rocks and of providing a good channel at all seasons. The other and more difficult task was that of devising some means by which the channel of the river at St. Louis could be saved from sand banks that were making navigation impossible on the western side of the stream.

Lee had no experience in dealing with currents and shoals, but he accepted the challenge of the mighty Mississippi. He went about his work in a most interesting manner. First he studied the problem on the ground and in the sullen river itself. Then he conferred with men who had wrestled with the same conditions before he had. From his own observations and with the advice of these engineers, he developed his plan. It was simple but it was sound. Starting from the eastern bank, he would construct a series of dykes which would throw the whole, tremendous weight of the Mississippi against the shoals that were choking navigation. He would make the river scour itself.

The plan was executed rapidly and was entirely successful, but when the work was nearly complete, it was halted because Congress failed to vote money to finish it. Residents of St. Louis were disgusted. Lee doubtless was disappointed, though he was trained as a soldier to obey orders without complaint. Promotion and new reputation were his. He had been made a First Lieutenant of Engineers in September, 1836, more than seven years after he first had been commissioned. Within less than two years from that time, he became Captain (August 7, 1838).

Lee was pleased, of course, to be a Captain of Engineers, which was high rank in a small corps, but he knew that he still would have a great deal of every-day hard work to do. He did it, did it conscientiously. Some of the still larger opportunities that were to open before him were created in the sand banks of the Mississippi, but these larger gains from the work at St. Louis were not immediately apparent. On the contrary, there was much more of dull, hard work. After a tour of inspection of forts on the coast of North Carolina, Captain Lee was sent in April, 1841, to repair some of the defences of New York Harbor. There he remained for five years, except for periods during which he was called to assist in the office of the Chief of Engineers in Washington.

Besides the burden of his official duties, Captain Lee had by this time the care of a family that was growing fast. His first child, a son named after Mr. Custis, had been born on September 16, 1832. About two years later, a girl arrived. She was named Mary. On May 31, 1837, the second son was born and was christened William Henry Fitzhugh, in honor of a loyal friend of the family who had counselled Mrs. Lee during the childhood of her brood. In June, 1839, the second daughter, Annie Carter Lee, was born, to be followed in less than two years by another girl, Eleanor Agnes, usually called Agnes. A third son, Robert Edward Lee, Jr., claimed a place in the family on

October 27, 1843. The fourth girl and seventh child, Mildred, was born early in 1846.

Captain Lee somewhat grimly welcomed these newcomers but he did not take in light mood the responsibility of rearing them. Every sickness of any of his children was an anxiety, each injury to them was an agony to him. Once, while the family was living in New York, the second boy, whom the other children called "Rooney," slipped off, climbed into a hayloft and did some experimenting with the cutting knife. In a few minutes he came home, screaming in pain, with the tips of two fingers almost severed. The surgeon of the post sewed them back in the hope that they would reknit, but the father suffered even more than did the son. For several nights Captain Lee remained by the bed of "Rooney" in order to be sure the boy did not undo the surgeon's work while tossing in sleep. Fortunately, to the infinite relief of a father who dreaded the maiming of any of his children, "Rooney" did not lose the fingertips.

Another time, at Arlington in winter, Captain Lee took Custis out for a walk in the snow. The youngster plodded along by his father's side for a time and then dropped behind. When Captain Lee looked back, Custis was struggling to walk in the tracks his father had made. "When I saw this," Lee told one of his friends long afterwards, "I said to myself, 'It behooves me to walk very straight when this fellow is already following in my tracks!'" That was the spirit in which he tried to rear his sons. He did not find it easy. The younger Lees were high-spirited lads and they did not learn quickly the code of self-discipline that was the first law of their father's life.

Lee's self-control had one unanticipated result in the summer of 1844. The old-time Board of Visitors of West Point had been abolished the previous year. Inspections were to be made and final examinations to be held under the eyes of a special army commission for that purpose by the President of the United States. Lee was appointed to the first of these commissions and for a fortnight was privileged to live at "The Point" in the company of some of the most distinguished of the country's soldiers.

Conspicuous among them by his dominating temper and his vast bulk was the commanding General of the Army, Major General Winfield Scott. He was six feet, five inches tall, weighed more than 230 pounds and often assumed a frowning, pompous manner, but he was an upright man and the ablest military leader of his day. For the General, whom he doubtless had seen often in Washington, Lee had much respect. Now he had opportunity every day of seeing Scott at close range.

Lee did not toady to the General. In one instance he differed squarely with Scott and prevailed on the commission to name his candidate for a faculty position at West Point in preference to the man Scott favored. This was done with so much courtesy that Scott was not angered. He watched Lee closely and perhaps critically as they sat together at the examination table, but if Lee observed this scrutiny, he remained himself—simple, kindly, courteous, and dignified. Scott wrote Lee's name on the tablets of his memory and, in less than two years, gave Lee an immensely greater opportunity than the Mississippi had offered.

This opportunity arose out of a violent turn in the long quarrel between the United States and Mexico over Texas, which had revolted against Mexico and had established its independence. In December, 1845, the Congress of the United States had admitted Texas to the Union and, in effect, had defied Mexico, which still claimed the State. Wise men on both sides of the border thought that war could be avoided, but the triumph of a pro-war party in Mexico led the government of that country to refuse to receive an American agent of peace. In April, 1846, troops of the two countries clashed, and in May they fought two sharp, small battles at Palo Alto and Reseca de la Palma. Before word of these two actions reached Washington, Congress declared war. Once that decision was reached, President James K. Polk, the cabinet, and the leading men of the army and navy decided that the surest way to win the war in the shortest possible time was to fight on Mexican soil.

Immediately, every soldier and every sailor of the United States asked himself the same question—"Am I going to Mexico?" All the officers attached to the regiments could assume that they would have a hand in the campaign against Mexico. They were few in number. Every one of them would be needed. It might not be so with staff officers, even with engineers. Captain Lee was as anxious as any man could be to have an active part in the war but he was not certain he would be sent to the front. When troops left Governor's Island for Mexico, he bade them farewell with positive envy. A month he waited, two months, three. Then at last, August 19, 1846, he received instructions to report at San Antonio, Texas, to Brigadier General John E. Wool. When Lee proceeded to obey those orders, he opened a new and intensely exciting chapter in his life.

CHAPTER FOUR

Lee's Adventures in Mexico

AFTER A JOURNEY of a month and two days, Captain Lee reached the quaint, half-Mexican city of San Antonio, Texas, and reported to his new commander, Brig. Gen. John E. Wool. The General had few engineers and he worked them hard. From the time of his arrival Lee was busy preparing for the march and then in showing inexperienced soldiers how to build bridges and to repair roads. With Wool's small army, Lee went to Monclava, Mexico, and then to Parras and to Encantada. The enemy offered no resistance.

Lee rode with a native guide across the wild country until, about nightfall, he saw twinkling lights on a hill beyond a little town. One glimpse of those lights was enough to frighten the guide: They were campfires, he said; the entire Mexican army was on that hill. They had better go back. Lee was not so easily satisfied. He told the guide to remain there while he went a little closer. Soon, on the high ground, through the gathering darkness, Lee dimly saw small white objects, which he took to be tents, but he was not quite sure. He rode through the town, which already was asleep, and then he cautiously approached the eminence. By this time he was in earshot. Shouts and laughter were audible. Still he walked his horse slowly forward, without any challenge from sentinels. In another moment he drew rein and probably laughed: What he had mistaken for tents were sheep; the "army" campfires had been lighted by herders who had stopped for the night on their way to market. They cordially greeted the young officer and told him that the Mexican army still was on the other side of the mountains. Lee thanked them, bade them good night, rode back to the American camp and reported to General Wool, but he had learned a new lesson in thoroughness: In reconnaissance, an officer must never assume what he cannot see.

Lee learned, almost at the same time and in a laughable manner that much depends, also, on the judgment of the man who sees. While Lee was on a visit to the headquarters of General Zachary Taylor, who commanded all the armies in that part of Mexico, a young officer galloped up and reported excitedly that 20,000 of the enemy with 250 pieces of artillery were advancing.

"Captain," said General Taylor quietly, "do you say you *saw* that force?"

"Yes, General," said the officer, who did not realize how much he was exaggerating.

"Captain," the General replied, "if you say you saw it, of course I must believe you; but I would not have believed it if I had seen it myself."

This was interesting. Many other things were instructive, also, but all the indications were that the decisive campaign of the war would be conducted much farther south in Mexico and by General Winfield Scott, rather than by General Zachary Taylor. Of course Lee wanted to be where the hardest fighting would occur. Consequently he was delighted when he received orders on the 17th of January, 1847, to proceed to the coast and to report to the chief engineer of the army.

Quickly Lee rode 250 miles to Brazos and joined the chief engineer, Col. Joseph G. Totten, who was calling to him some of the ablest men of the engineering corps. One of them was Lee's old-time West Point chum, Joseph E. Johnston. Another was a handsome, dark, young

Louisianian, with the eye of an eagle. Pierre G. T. Beauregard was his name. Still another was a brilliant red-headed lieutenant, George B. McClellan of Pennsylvania, who had been graduated second in the class of 1846 at West Point.

After a tedious month at Brazos, Lee was assigned to Scott's own ship, aboard which the commanding General welcomed gladly the Captain with whom he had spent pleasant days at the Military Academy in 1844. Soon Scott began to discuss his plans with Lee and before many weeks, he admitted Lee to the circle of confidential military advisers that he called his "little cabinet."

On the 5th of March, 1847, Scott arrived off the port of Vera Cruz, which United States warships already were blockading. Immediately every soldier and every seaman could guess what was going to happen next: General Scott intended to land and capture Vera Cruz. In his own mind, Scott had even bolder plans. If the occupation of the main port of their country did not lead the Mexicans to ask for peace, he would move inland and perhaps would undertake to march to their capital, slightly more than 200 miles from the coast.

The landings were ordered to be made south of Vera Cruz, March 9, on the open beach. When the designated hour arrived, crowded surf boats left the side of each large vessel. As the craft approached the shore, observers on the ships expected to see gun fire break out from the sand dunes. Losses in landing, it was feared, would be heavy, though each man looked as if he were resolved to get ashore even if he died on the beach. Soon the boats were within musket range. Every man held his breath—but not one shot was fired. A few minutes later, the Stars and Stripes were flying from the highest dune, and the first "wave" was spreading out to cope with any surprise the enemy might offer.

Reconnaissance showed that the Mexicans had taken refuge in Vera

Cruz and in the castle of San Juan d'Ulloa, which was about 1,000 yards offshore. This fortress was constructed of a coral-like limestone, was protected by reefs on three sides, and was supposed to be heavily armed. Vera Cruz itself was surrounded by a wall, outside which were many prickly pear bushes and numbers of man-traps. These traps were holes in the ground with a sharp stake at the bottom of each.

After examining all this, General Scott had to decide whether he would send his whole army forward and try to capture Vera Cruz by storm, or whether he would lay siege to it, batter down a part of the wall and enter the city through the breach if the Mexicans refused to surrender. In the "little cabinet," when these alternatives were discussed, all agreed that it would be less expensive in life to take the city by siege than by storm.

Officers were named immediately to reconnoiter the approaches and to decide where the American batteries should be placed. Lee was one of those selected for this work. Lieutenant Beauregard was another. On the 19th of March, these two were returning from the front along a narrow path that had been cut through the thick brush. As they came to a turn in the path, a sentinel's challenge suddenly rang out: "Who goes there?"

"Friends," Lee shouted.

"Officers," yelled Beauregard.

Before the words had left their lips, the excited sentinel fired point blank at Lee. The bullet passed between the inside of the arm and the skin of the upper chest. If the soldier had been a better marksman by two inches, the history of the War between the States might have been different. As it was, Lee escaped all injury.

With utmost energy, Lee and his brother-engineers erected batteries. Lee soon realized, as did others, that the cannon of the army were not powerful enough to breach the walls and to silence the Mexican artillery. Heavier guns had to be brought from the warships. To get these ashore and then to pull them through the deep sand was a stern task, but at length it was performed. Sailors under their own naval officers were detailed to serve the guns. They did so most acceptably but they complained much, because they did not like to fill sandbags and to fight behind them. A naval captain later explained to Lee: "I knew we would have no use for dirt banks on shipboard, that there what we want is clear decks and open sea." Then he added: "And the fact is, Captain, I don't like this land fighting anyway. It ain't clean."

After the naval batteries went into action, the wall of Vera Cruz soon was so battered that the garrison asked for terms. Scott agreed to permit the Mexicans to march out with flags flying, to lay down their arms, and to make a pledge not to fight again until exchanged for American prisoners. All these conditions were met. Vera Cruz was occupied.

As the Mexican government still gave no evidence of a purpose to make peace, General Scott boldly determined to start a march on Mexico City. This advance commenced on April 12 and soon brought the American army to the small River del Plan. Beyond that stream, the only road fit for artillery and wagons made a steady ascent through the foothills of the mountains to Jalapa, which was about twenty-seven miles farther inland and at an elevation of 4,500 feet. The country near the river was so rough that the road left the bank and wound on a curve to the North for a distance of about three miles before it came back to the watercourse. Close to the point where the road returned to the river bank, there was a high ridge, shaped much like a cone and known as Cerro Gordo (Thick Ridge). The ground between the river and this ridge was called the Pass of Cerro Gordo. It was so narrow that if American troops entered it, they would have to press straight on in the face of a Mexican battery of six guns that could be fired directly at them.

To find a way of getting around this obstacle, General Scott sent out Lee and other engineers. With only one soldier as a companion, Lee mounted one and then another of the successive ravines north of the river. He satisfied himself, from what he saw of the ground, that the army could cut trails along which it could get beyond Cerro Gordo without having to storm the pass. Farther on, he reasoned, the troops would be able to get into the Jalapa Road.

Presently, climbing higher, Lee came to a large spring in a beautiful setting of lofty trees and underbrush of glistening green. He had encountered no Mexicans as he had made his way through the brush, but now, while he was admiring the scene, he heard voices close at hand. Men, talking in Spanish, were coming to the spring.

Captain Lee did not have time to get away. If he was to escape, he must hide. His quick, observant glance showed him only one refuge —the shrub-covered side of a great fallen tree. Instantly he slipped under it. Scarcely had he put the bushes back in place before soldiers were all around him. They drank from the spring, loafed, talked, sauntered around and several times barely missed stepping on him. Other Mexicans came while the first group still lingered. Once used, the spring was never deserted. Lee had to remain there, absolutely motionless and defenceless against so many adversaries. His companion was having a similar experience in a like shelter near at hand. That afternoon probably was the longest in the life of Robert Lee. Not until darkness fell were he and his comrade able to creep out and to back down the ravine.

The result was worth the hardship. Information supplied by Lee and various other engineers made it possible for General Scott to send troops around the northern end of Cerro Gordo to attack the enemy's camp and to seize the Jalapa road. Two other columns attacked the same days, April 17–18, and quickly drove the enemy from his stronghold.

This Battle of Cerro Gordo was Captain Lee's first action in open country, precisely as the siege of Vera Cruz had been his first attack on a fixed position. In the midst of the struggle, Lee came upon a pathetic scene. Near a hut, a Mexican boy with a shattered arm was lying under a dying soldier. The lad, who probably was a drummer, was too much weakened to lift the weight of the man from him. A little girl was by the side of the two, but could not help the wounded boy. Lee of course had the dying man lifted and had litter bearers carry him and the wounded boy to a field-hospital. Then Lee turned to the girl: "Her large black eyes were streaming with tears," he wrote, "her hands crossed over her breast; her hair in one long plait behind reached almost to her waist, her shoulders and arms bare, and without stockings or shoes." Lee added: "Her plaintive tone of 'mil gracias, Señor,' still lingers in my ear."

Near that hut and everywhere around Cerro Gordo, Lee found a battlefield as horrible a sight as he thought it would be, but he realized that he could act promptly under fire. That is something of which no man can be sure until he has met the test of actual warfare. Lee sustained the test without being unnerved. He recalled later while the bloody fight was being waged, he had found himself wondering where he would have put Custis if the boy had been with him. After the battle, Lee wrote his wife: "I endeavored to give thanks to our Heavenly Father for all his mercies to me, for his preservation of me through all the dangers I have passed, and [for] all the blessings he has bestowed upon me, for I know I fell far short of my obligations."

From Cerro Gordo the army advanced on April 19th to Jalapa and later marched ninety miles southwestward to Puebla, on the road to

Mexico City. At Puebla, Scott waited long for reinforcements and supplies which he thought President Polk was not moving as rapidly as would have been practicable. The General sometimes was furious and sometimes bitter over this, but he always was careful to see that his troops were kept busy and that his officers were instructed. In the evenings he would gather around him some of the most promising of the younger men and would talk to them at length of whatever military problems had arisen during the day. These nightly conferences at General Scott's headquarters were an important part of the military education of Captain Robert Lee. The particular duty of the younger engineer at Puebla was to take the few existing maps and to collect additional information from all persons who would supply it. On this basis, he made a better map.

Study of the ground showed that if General Scott intended to go from Puebla to Mexico City, he had first to cross a range of lofty mountains that might be strongly fortified near the crest. When these mountains were passed, Scott would descend to the great plateau which has an elevation of about 7,400 feet. Then, as he came nearer the capital, he would have to traverse a country of shallow lakes, of narrow raised roads (causeways) and of troublesome hills that would shelter all the artillery the enemy could mass. Finally, if Scott was to advance from Puebla to Mexico, he must give up all hope of keeping troops along the route from Vera Cruz to Jalapa and on to Puebla and Mexico City. He would not have sufficient men to fight and to guard that long road. In military language, he would be forced to abandon his lines of supply and to get food for his troops from the country through which he was passing.

Such difficulties as these would have deterred a weak man and would have made a man of average courage hesitate. General Scott accepted difficulty as a spur and danger as a challenge. He waited only for a few more soldiers. On the 7th of August, Gen. Franklin Pierce arrived at Puebla with 2,500 additional troops, who raised the total at General Scott's command to 10,738. With these, on August 8, Scott started for Mexico City. Two days later, the column crossed the crest of the mountains without opposition and looked down on the magnificent country that surrounds the capital. General Scott himself subsequently wrote: "Recovering from the sublime trance, probably not a man in the column failed to say to his neighbor or himself: That splendid city soon shall be ours!"

When the column reached the town of Ayotla, nineteen miles from Mexico City, the difficulty of a direct approach to the capital seemed greater than ever. The only road led along a narrow causeway between two lakes. This causeway ran under a strongly fortified hill of 300 feet, known as El Peñón. General Scott believed his men would be able to take this eminence in the face of fire of the Mexican soldiers, but he knew the battle would cost many lives. He was pleased, therefore, when some of his officers reported that they had made a profitable reconnaissance in another direction. They had satisfied themselves that it would be easier to capture Mexico City by going around the southern end of two nearby lakes.

Scott accepted this report and promptly took his army to the village of San Agustín. Here he found another obstacle in his way. From the village, the road ran North to a ranch named San Antonio, where the Mexicans had planted cannon. This artillery would kill many Americans if Scott attempted to advance up the road. He could not reach San Antonio by going East of the road, because the ground there was too marshy. West of the road there was a vast field of old lava—pedregal, from a long-dead volcano. This pedregal was so rough that wagons and artillery might not be able to move over it. In other words, there did not appear to be any direct way of getting to San Antonio, and from San Antonio to Mexico City.

What was Scott to do? His engineers, Lee among them, asked the natives about other roads. Almost directly West of San Agustín, at a distance of two miles, the officers were told, there was another road called the San Angel. This ran North for some distance and then turned East and joined the main road above San Antonio. If the United States troops could get over to the San Angel road, they might be able to pass San Antonio without having to fight for it.

To see whether the army could get from San Agustín to the San Angel road, General Scott sent Captain Lee on the 18th of August across the pedregal. Along the southern edge of the lava, Lee soon discovered an old trail which he felt sure the engineers could make smooth enough for wagons and artillery to pass. As he approached the western side of the pedregal, Lee ran into a few Mexican soldiers. They did not stop to fight or to parley. As quickly as they could, they disappeared westward. Lee continued his reconnaissance. At length, when he climbed to the high ground called Zacatepec—it resembled a little volcano—he could look over to the San Angel road and could see many more Mexicans there.

Lee went back to San Agustín and told Scott that the San Angel road existed and that the army could get to the vicinity of it but probably would have to fight to reach and to hold it. The General discussed plans that night and, on the 19th, sent Lee with about 600 men to build a road across the pedregal. A considerable part of the infantry went along to protect the road-makers. In this force were a number of young men besides Captain Lee who were to make a name for themselves in future years. One of the most inconspicuous of them at the time was an artillery Lieutenant, 23 years of age, who had been graduated the previous year at West Point. This tall, solemn-faced young fellow, who was secretly as ambitious as he manifestly was awkward, bore the name of Thomas Jonathan Jackson. He will be heard from many times in later chapters of this book.

Early in the afternoon, while the construction of the road was proceeding well, the United States troops came within range of Mexican soldiers who were on the western side of the San Angel road, at a place called Padierna. The American commanders soon saw that the way to deal with these Mexicans was to move part of the troops silently into the pedregal, and march them through it until they were northeast of the end or the flank of the line the Mexicans had formed. When this was done, the Americans could move quietly westward, get behind the Mexicans and drive them off. The first part of this advance was easy, but when the Americans got to the western side of the San Angel road, they found another and larger body of hostile troops still farther North. In other words, the United States soldiers were between two forces of their enemy. Fortunately, the Mexicans did not realize that the Americans, who numbered 3,300, were cut off from those of their comrades who remained in the pedregal east of the San Angel road. If the Mexicans had understood the situation and had attacked at the same time from the north and from the south, they could have wiped out the Americans.

Those United States officers who talked with Captain Lee about this situation did not believe the Mexicans would attack from both sides. The Americans reasoned, on the contrary, that if they beat the troops at Padierna, south of them, the Mexicans to the north would not stand. An assault on the village from the rear would be much easier if the enemy could be deceived into thinking the main attack was coming from some other direction. East of the road there were sufficient troops to make a pretence of advancing on Padierna. The difficulty was in having the necessary orders given these American regiments by General Scott, who was supposed to be at Zacatepec.

As soon as Captain Lee heard the generals express a wish to send a message to Scott, he offered to take it. A storm was raging at the time. The approaching night promised to be impenetrably black except when lightning flashed. Lee had been across that part of the pedregal only once. In getting back to Zacatepec, he would have to rely on his sense of direction. If he encountered a Mexican outpost he might be killed. The cause justified the risk. Given the message and an escort of a few brave men, Lee started at once. Darkness overtook him before he could get across the San Angel road. He and his companions had to feel their way, almost step by step, along the treacherous, uneven lava field. When they approached the American outpost, they had to make sure they were recognized as friends and not fired upon as enemies.

At last Lee reached Zacatepec, but Scott was not at the advanced headquarters. He had gone back to San Agustín. Lee did not hesitate: the lives of other men were at stake. Tired as he was, he must proceed to San Agustín. Thanks to his excellent physical condition, which no fast living ever had weakened, Lee got to the village and found Scott, still awake and at work. The General saw immediately that the plan for the attack on Padierna was a good one and he at once prepared to have the regiments in the pedregal act as if they intended to attack in front of the Mexicans beyond the San Angel road.

Soon two of Scott's generals appeared and expressed a desire to return to their troops who were around Zacatepec. Scott decided to keep one of the generals with him but sent the other back. As that officer, General David Twiggs, had injured his foot, Lee felt that he should accompany him instead of taking a few hours' rest at headquarters. Twiggs and Lee probably went on horseback, but the ride was an ordeal, because this was Lee's third journey across the pedregal in twenty-four hours. Two of the three crossings were in darkness. When General Scott came to write of this in his report of the campaign, he said it was "the greatest feat of physical and moral courage performed by any individual, in my knowledge, pending the campaign."

On the 20th of August, the demonstration was made east of the San Angel road. Precisely as the Americans had hoped, it diverted the attention of the enemy at Padierna. The Mexicans were attacked in the rear and were routed amid so much excitement that the troops north of the American position yielded to panic and ran away. This Battle of Padierna—or as the Americans called it, Contreras—was followed that same day by a struggle at Churubusco, where the crossroad from San Angel joined the main road from San Agustín past San Antonio. There again the Mexicans were defeated.

These two actions of August 20, 1847, were followed on the 24th by an armistice which lasted until the 7th of September. Then the Mexicans insisted on terms almost as stiff as they could have demanded if they had won the war. Regretfully General Scott had to renew the campaign. After a bloody action at Molino del Rey on September 8, the Americans on the 13th captured the castle and hill of Chapultepec. When this was in American hands, the occupation of Mexico City was easy. Formal peace was not signed until February 2, 1848, but all the important fighting was over.

So little did the American commanders have to do that they now began to quarrel among themselves. Captain Lee, of course, supported his chief, General Scott, but he met with so little success as a conciliator he might have repeated to some of the quarreling officers an amusing plea General Twiggs made to a staff officer. This young soldier, who had been sent to give a certain order, came back to explain that he had not delivered it because he had found conditions different from those that General Twiggs had assumed. As the officer began to argue the matter, Twiggs interrupted him. "Captain," he said, "I know that you can prove you are right, and that my order was wrong; in fact, you gentlemen are always right, but for God's sake do wrong sometimes." Lee might have asked that some of the disputing officers admit they might be in the wrong. They were in no temper to do so. Several of the seniors tried to convince the American nation that they had been the men responsible for the victory and that they had been cheated of the credit due them.

None of the younger officers of the army had done more than Captain Lee to win the campaign and none received more conspicuous recognition. Before the autumn of 1848, he was promoted Major, then Lieutenant Colonel and then Colonel, "by brevet." This meant that he had the higher honorary title, as a reward of valor, though he remained at his former level of pay and kept his regular rank of Captain. Along with these brevets, he had praise in the reports of virtually all the Generals under whom he served in Mexico. Scott's high opinion was confirmed and deepened. He said many times that Lee was the most promising of junior American soldiers. Lee himself would have been the last person to magnify what he had done in Mexico. He had shown his endurance, and his ability to think clearly and to act promptly under fire. Many lessons in the command of men and in the management of battles he had learned from that able teacher, Winfield Scott; but Lee was not the braggart type to exalt his own part in the struggle. He had nothing in common with those who, after every struggle, bore their friends with the most tedious military narrative in the world—the story of "how I won the war."

With gratitude to God for the service he had been able to render and for the perils he had escaped, Brevet Colonel Lee left Vera Cruz about the end of the first week of June, 1848, on a steamer that docked at New Orleans. From that city he ascended the Mississippi River and then the Ohio to Wheeling, Virginia, where he took train for Washington. He reached the capital on the 29th of June, about a year and ten months after he had left for the war.

He had written often and affectionately while he had been away and had informed the family of his plans of arrival. At Arlington, where Mrs. Lee and her children were living with her parents, there was the liveliest excitement over his coming. At last from the portico he was seen as he approached on a hired horse. A carriage had been sent for him but in some way its driver had failed to find him.

The instant Lee dismounted, everyone observed that he was getting gray and that he showed the results of his campaigning but, of course, there were kisses and embraces and happy greetings. While Mrs. Lee, the girls and the older sons were half laughing and half crying for joy, the Colonel asked, "Where is my little boy?" As he spoke his eye lighted on a youngster, whom he lifted at once and held to his face. A shout went up from all the portico. Another little boy standing nearby looked hurt and puzzled. The Colonel had not recognized his own son, Robert, Junior, and had picked up and embraced a neighbor's visiting child.

CHAPTER FIVE

Lee Faces the Great Tragedy

As soon as he had renewed acquaintance with his youngest boy, Colonel Lee resumed his peace-time duties. After some work in the Office of the Chief of Engineers during the summer of 1848, Lee was assigned on August 13 to construct Fort Carroll, on a shoal half way between the harbor of Baltimore, Maryland and the mouth of the Patapsco River. This labor of nearly four years had some interest for Lee, though much of it was routine of the sort he had performed before the Mexican War. Lee's next assignment was one usually regarded as a "plum," a high, easy honor: In 1852 he was named Superintendent of the Military Academy and was directed to report there in September.

His response may have surprised the War Department. Instead of accepting the honor gladly, he asked that he be given some other duty. He said that he lacked the "skill and experience" required for the administration of the Academy and, in his heart of hearts, he did not want to have to take on his heart the burden of guiding so many young men. With three sons of his own, he knew how much that responsibility tested him and he did not think he could do all that would be required for the entire corps.

Because of its confidence in him the War Department would not cancel his orders. In the early autumn of 1852, he entered on his duties earnestly but with continuing doubt of his ability to do all he should. Lee's "sympathy with young people," the Secretary of War had to admit, "was rather an impediment than a qualification for the superintendency."

One change that came to Lee during the time he was at the Academy was a deepening of his sense of dependence on Almighty God. He had been baptized in the Episcopal Church as a little child, but he had never been confirmed. During the Mexican War, when death had seemed near to him, God had been nearer. Lee had come back from the war with a deep belief in a God who "doeth all things well." Now that he was in charge of some of the nation's finest young men, he felt that he should confess the faith that was in him and should ally himself with the church. By the side of two of his daughters he was confirmed July 17, 1853. The rite was not to be performed and forgotten. It represented an avowed allegiance that remained first in his heart.

He needed all his faith, because, as he told Jefferson Davis, some of "the cadets did exceedingly worry" him. Fitzhugh Lee, his own nephew, son of his beloved brother Smith, was twice brought close to dismissal during the time Colonel Lee was Superintendent. A strange cadet called "Curly" Whistler stood first in drawing but almost completely disdained to study the subjects he did not like. "Curly" was given numerous chances but, in the end was sent home. He became famous as the artist James McNeill Whistler, whose portrait of his mother is one of his best known works. The artist was always proud of West Point and a defender of Colonel Lee.

Lee's method of dealing with cadets of honor and character was displayed many times and never in circumstances more unusual than those that involved Cadet Archibald Gracie Jr. of New York. One afternoon on parade, Gracie, who was of powerful frame, amused himself by stepping on the heels of Wharton Green who was marching directly in front of him. Wharton naturally got mad and said that

Gracie was going to get a beating. "Not from you," said Gracie. As soon as the formation was dismissed, Green went up to Gracie, struck at him and started a furious fight. Gracie was getting the worse of it when the fencing instructor came up, stopped the battle, accosted Gracie, and demanded his name and class. While the faculty-member was taking these down, Green calmly walked away. When the instructor asked Gracie with whom he was fighting, the cadet answered, "You will have to ask him, for I'm no informer." The New York boy was put under arrest and, of course, was reported to the Superintendent. Lee had the papers on his desk the next morning when Cadet Green entered and saluted. "Colonel Lee," he began seriously, "Mr. Gracie was yesterday reported for fighting on the parade ground, and the 'other fellow' was not."

"Yes, sir," said Lee, "and I presume you are 'the other fellow.' "

"I am, sir," said Green, "and I wish to submit the case in full for your consideration. Don't you think it very hard on him, Colonel, after getting the worse of the fracas, to have to take all of the penalty?"

"Admitted," said the Superintendent, "what then?"

"Simply this, sir. Whatever punishment is meted out to him, I insist on having the same given to me."

"The offence entails a heavy penalty."

"I am aware of the fact, Colonel, but Mr. Gracie is not entitled to a monopoly of it."

Lee smiled: "No sir; you will get neither report nor penalty for this, and neither will Mr. Gracie get the latter. I will cancel the report. Don't you think, Mr. Green, that it is better for brothers to dwell together in peace and harmony?"

"Yes, Colonel, and if we were all like you, it would be an easy thing to do."

Eleven years later, in the ghastly trenches of Petersburg, Lee visited the lines held by some Alabama troops. In his desire to see what the enemy was doing, Lee forgot that the trenches were so close together and so intently watched by sharpshooters that a man who showed any part of the body over the top of the trenches was certain to get a shot and almost certain to receive a wound. Incautiously Lee stepped up on the firestep of the trench within sight of the enemy. Instantly a young General sprang between him and the sharpshooters to protect him. It was Archibald Gracie.

In the company of such fine young men in 1852–55 there was relief sometimes from the burden of responsibility for their well being; but, on the whole, Lee was not happy as Superintendent. He wished to do work for which he felt better qualified, and, as said once in another connection, he wanted to enjoy the "cordiality and friendship in the army" that were "the great attraction of the service."

After two years and a half, his desire was realized. Because of Indian depredations, Congress provided early in 1855 for two new regiments of infantry and two of cavalry. The Secretary of War, Jefferson Davis, was anxious to have these new regiments under the best procurable officers, and he was aware, no doubt, that Lee was restless at West Point. The position of Lieutenant Colonel in the Second Cavalry was, for these reasons, offered Lee. The engineers were, of course, Lee's first love but he still was a Captain on the active list though a Brevet Colonel because of his service in Mexico. His old ambition to advance in his profession remained as firm as it had been when he was at West Point. He believed he had a better chance of further promotion with the cavalry than with the engineers, and, to repeat, he was anxious to be relieved of duty as Superintendent.

For these reasons, he accepted the new appointment, left the Academy March 31, 1855, took his family back to Arlington, and then proceeded to Louisville, Kentucky, where the new cavalry regiment was being organized. Lee reached Louisville April 20th and began a service which was necessary in the life of an army but in many ways was hard, unpleasant and lonely.

Because he was fair-minded as well as intelligent and patient, he often was named to act a member of a court—"court martial," it was styled—to pass on charges against officers and soldiers. This carried him to stations as far apart as Fort Riley, Kansas, and Carlisle Barracks, Pennsylvania, before his regiment was ordered to Texas. After he joined the troops again at Fort Cooper, on the Comanche reserve in Texas, he had still more court martial duty that involved long travel and the hearing of disputed testimony on complicated charges. Even at Camp Cooper, which was remote from "the beaten track," Lee had to serve on courts. Once, in doing so, he found himself called on to provide food for Mrs. George H. Thomas, the wife of Major Thomas, another member of the court. Lee wrote amusingly of this experience: "The major can fare as I do, but I fear she will fare badly, because my man Kumer is both awkward and unskilled. I can, however, give them plently of bread and of beef, but with the exception of preserved vegetables, fruits, etc., I can give them very little else. I sent yesterday to the settlements below and got a few eggs, some butter, and one old hen. I shall not reflect upon her. . . ."

The officers at Camp Cooper who tried to eat the hen that Lee declined to libel in his letter were men of ability and, in general, of good nature; but they were spread too thin, when court was not in session, to afford much companionship for one another or adequate instruction for the men in the ranks. Sometimes at Camp Cooper and at other isolated stations in Texas, Lee had only the company of a captain or two and perhaps three or four young lieutenants. One of these junior officers at Camp Cooper, a magnificently handsome young blond, was Lieut. John B. Hood. He was awkward and a bit crude but evidently a young man with a promise of a future. In the loneliness of the vast spaces of Texas, John Hood's craving for the company of girls led him to make long rides to the scattered homes of the few humble pioneers who happened to have daughters. Colonel Lee observed that Hood was visiting one of these homes with frequency and he began to fear that the young man might marry a crude, illiterate girl. It was not proper, of course, for Lee to say, "You must not marry" or even to say, "You shall not go to that house"; but with the tact that sprang from his innate consideration of the feelings of other persons, he turned one of their conversations to the general subject of marriage and said after a time, "Never marry unless you can do so into a family that will enable your children to feel proud of both sides of the house." Hood had sense enough to take the hint. When next he appears in these pages, as one of the most promising soldiers of the South, he will be still a bachelor.

Life was undeniably and incurably dull on the Texas frontier. Aside from court martials and the routine of an isolated little army post, Colonel Lee had only one adventure—a long search for some Indians who had been stealing cattle and making trouble on the edge of the Staked Plains. With four squadrons of cavalry, Lee pursued the redmen but, at the end of forty days, he returned to Camp Cooper without having encountered any natives. Another column had met a party of four and had killed two of them.

In October, 1857, a break came in this drab life, but it was a break that had sorrow behind it. Mrs. Custis, the mother of Mrs. Lee, had died in April, 1853, while the Lees were at West Point. "She was to me," said Colonel Lee sadly, "all that a mother could be." Mr. Custis survived her for about four years and a half and then he, too, came to his end. When word of this reached Colonel Lee in Texas, he reflected sadly that Mrs. Lee had no near kinsmen who could advise her on financial matters. Both of Lee's older sons, Custis and "Rooney," were officers in the army and had distant posts. The Colonel himself must go back to Virginia to transact family business. Leave was extended promptly and generously by the ranking officer. Lee hurried to Washington where he arrived on the 11th of November. It was a sad home-coming. Arlington did not seem the same without its venerable owner; the life of the plantation was disorganized; worst of all, Mrs. Lee had been so crippled by arthritis during her husband's long absence from home that she now was virtually an invalid, an old woman at 49. It took all of Colonel Lee's courage and all his faith in God to reconcile him to this.

Under Mr. Custis's will, Lee was one of four executors of the estate, but the other three declined to qualify. The entire task of settling the affairs of the old gentleman, who had been notoriously negligent in business, fell to the lot of his son-in-law. Mr. Custis had left Arlington and adjoining property to Mrs. Lee for life and had divided his other plantations between "Rooney" and young Robert. On the death of Mrs. Lee, Arlington was to belong to Custis Lee. To each of his three grand-daughters, Mr. Custis left $10,000. How this money was to be provided, his will did not make altogether clear. Besides, he owed $10,000 when he died and had made provision for the emancipation of his slaves within five years.

The troubles Colonel Lee had in untangling this will were a lesson to him of the obligation every man has to "keep his house in order." To raise the money for the payment of debts and for the repair of neglected Arlington, Colonel Lee had to ask for a long leave of absence from the army and then for another and still another to a total of more than two years. Even then, the closest attention to the property was scarcely enough to bring it slowly to a better condition. The one gratification of the whole task was the fine attitude of Custis Lee.

When he found that his father's time and money were being spent on Arlington, he generously had a deed drawn by which he gave to his father everything his Grandfather Custis had left him. Of course Colonel Lee would not accept this, but he had much satisfaction in knowing that Custis appreciated what he was trying to do for the estate.

In the midst of this labor to make Arlington self-sustaining, Colonel Lee received on the 17th of October, 1859, an order to report immediately to the War Department. Without waiting even to put on his uniform, he rode to Washington and learned that he had been designated to command a force of marines who were being sent in haste to Harpers Ferry, Virginia. Some sort of an insurrection had broken out there—the War Department at the moment did not know precisely what it was. Colonel Lee must go there by train with the marines and must restore order.

Lee went. What he found at the junction of the Potomac and the Shenandoah was the so-called "John Brown raid." The fanatic John Brown, a native of New York, 59 years of age, who long had been an anti-slavery agitator in Kansas, had undertaken with a few followers to induce the slaves around Harpers Ferry to rise against their masters. Brown had taken a few hostages and had tried to seize the United States arsenal at Harpers Ferry, but he had been compelled to take refuge in the fire-engine house, where he was barricaded. Colonel Lee's duty was to arrest Brown and his followers. This was done promptly by breaking down the engine-house door and seizing the insurrectionists after they had refused to surrender. Lee placed Brown in the hands of the Virginia officers of the law and soon returned to Washington. "The result," he wrote in his report, "proves that the plan was the attempt of a fanatic or a madman." This was said without any knowledge that Brown's mother and her mother and several of their kin had suffered from insanity. Lee simply judged Brown by the man's acts and did not attempt to indict the entire North for the crime of Brown, though, of course, Lee shared the resentment of the South over the evidence that Brown had the financial backing and the moral support of several of the leading anti-slavery spokesmen of the North.

After testifying in the congressional investigation of the John Brown raid, Colonel Lee once more went to Texas to rejoin his regiment. He arrived in February, 1860, and for a time acted as commander of the Department of Texas. In that position he had to deal with a troublesome border bandit by the name of Juan Cortinas, but he soon found in Texas something unspeakably worse than the thievery of Cortinas. Sectional hate was rising between the North and the South over the demand of some Northerners for the abolition of slavery. Most Southerners insisted that slavery was recognized in the constitution of the United States and that Congress could not abolish slavery or keep slave owners from taking their slaves with them into territories that had not been organized into States. Only the States, said these Southerners, could put an end to slavery. Some of the abolitionists admitted that the Constitution recognized slavery, but they asserted this was a reason for condemning the Constitution and not a reason for acquiescing in slavery. In 1843 the abolitionist leader, William Lloyd Garrison, had urged that the North leave a union that had a constitution which was "a covenant with death and an agreement with hell." At Framingham, Massachusetts in 1854, Garrison had publicly burned a printed copy of the Constitution and had cried, "So perish all compromises with tyranny!" William H. Seward, a man of greater capacity than Garrison, had spoken in 1850 of a "higher law than the Constitution" and in 1858, at Rochester, he had said that the struggle over slavery was "an irrepressible conflict." The more vehement Southerners met these statements with answers equally extreme and they protested that the destruction of the Constitution was the aim of Northerners. The South, they said, was trying to "preserve the Constitution." If this could not be done, the Southern States should secede from the Union and, if need be, set up a new joint government of the States in which slavery was lawful.

This was not the universal view. Neither the North nor the South was of one mind. All shades of opinion prevailed. Some Northerners believed that a State had the right to withdraw from the Union; some Southerners denied this. Hundreds of thousands in free as well as in slave States believed that secession was not a right, but that if any of the States did leave the Union they should not be punished for doing so or be made to return to the Union. Many Southerners conceded that the union of the States was meant to be permanent, but they gave warning that if there were attempted coercion of the seceding States for their leaving the Union, those States should and would defend themselves.

In general, Southern men who were the sons or grandsons of strong Federalists were "old-line Whigs" or "Union men" in 1860 and did not admit the right of secession. "Southern Whigs" believed that the States had a right to leave the Union but should not do so unless they had extreme provocation. Many Democrats believed in the right of secession and stood ready to vote for their States to leave the Union if Congress did anything to interfere with slavery. A few Southern Democrats upheld the right of secession in theory but said that the preservation of the Union was important.

Where citizens of a republic are divided in opinion, it sometimes happens that men who have extreme, convinced views are those who take the lead. Persons of moderate, open mind see both sides of the question and will not move until they are shoved. Extremists do the shoving. It was so in 1860. One extreme was represented by Democrats who came from agricultural States where slaves were worked profitably. These men were convinced believers in the rights of the States,

Photos by Wayne Andrews

STRATFORD, WESTMORELAND COUNTY, WHERE LEE WAS BORN

ARLINGTON, LEE'S HOME AFTER HIS MARRIAGE

and they were ready to secede and to resist the North if the government of the United States passed into the hands of abolitionists who might undertake to coerce the South. At the other extreme were those of the abolitionists who believed that slavery must be ended at any price and that if the Southern States attempted to leave the Union in order to preserve slavery, war should be made on those States.

As 1860 was a year for the election of a new President, this deep division of angry, unreasoning opinion led to the nomination of four candidates. Whigs of moderate mind named John Bell of Tennessee as their candidate. Union Democrats selected Stephen A. Douglas of Illinois. Republicans chose Abraham Lincoln of the same state. Southern Democrats picked John C. Breckinridge. With so many candidates in the field it was almost certain that the man with the largest electoral vote would represent a minority, not a majority of the voters. The next President might be the candidate of an extremist minority.

With that prospect before him, every American of 1860 had to decide which side he would take and what he would do if secession or a dissolution of the Union followed the election. In Texas, Colonel Lee found that most of the people were for secession in the event of the election of the Republican candidate, Abraham Lincoln. Lee himself did not talk of politics often, but he had clear opinions. When the election resulted in the choice of Lincoln by forty-two per cent of the participating voters, Lee did not change his opinions. Nor was he moved when South Carolina and Mississippi, Florida, Alabama and Georgia voted to secede from the Union. On January 23, 1861, when secession still was spreading, Colonel Lee wrote this in a letter that was probably addressed to his son Custis:

> The South, in my opinion, has been aggrieved by the acts of the North, as you say. I feel the aggression, and am willing to take every proper step for redress. It is the principle I contend for, not individual or private gain. As an American citizen, I take great pride in my coun-

try, her prosperity and institutions, and would defend any State if her rights were invaded. But I anticipate no greater calamity for the country than a dissolution of the Union. It would be an accumulation of all the evils we complain of, and I am willing to sacrifice everything but honor for its preservation. I hope, therefore, that all constitutional means will be exhausted before there is a recourse to force. Secession is nothing but revolution. The framers of our Constitution never exhausted so much labor, wisdom and forebearance in its formation, and surrounded it with so many guards and securities, if it was intended to be broken by every member of the Confederacy at will. . . . Still, a Union that can only be maintained by swords and bayonets, and in which strife and civil war are to take the place of brotherly love and kindness, has no charm for me. I shall mourn for my country and for the welfare and progress of mankind. If the Union is dissolved, and the Government disrupted, I shall return to my native State and share the miseries of my people, and save in defence will draw my sword on none.

There he stood. Nobody who talked with him in Texas at the time had any doubt regarding his position. He believed secession was nothing more nor less than revolution, and that the occasion for it had not come. If secession was a tragic reality, he would side with his State, because, as he said, he always had been taught to believe, and did believe that his first obligations were due Virginia. He had confidence that Virginia would not act on impulse, but would proceed deliberately, as she had in the past, and would seek every honorable means of avoiding civil war. If she failed and determined to secede, he would go with her; and if she were assailed, he would defend her.

The test came quickly. In February, 1861, he received orders to proceed at once to Washington and to report to the Secretary of War. No explanation was given, no intimation of the reason for this sudden summons.

CHAPTER SIX

Lee Supports His Mother State

AFTER REACHING Washington, March 1, 1861, Lee reported to Scott and talked privately for three hours with the General. Of what passed between them, neither ever said a word afterwards. It is probable that Scott said he wished Lee to be near at hand in the crisis that was developing over secession. Possibly, also, Scott gave a hint of early promotion for Lee and intimated that if he found himself physically unable to take the field at the head of the United States army, he would want Lee as his second in command. This is conjecture. Nothing is known positively, except that, at the close of their conversation, Lee was told to remain in or near Washington where he would be accessible if needed.

There followed seven of the most tragic weeks America ever knew. On the 4th, Abraham Lincoln took the oath as President and delivered an inaugural that deepened the dispute. To some, the attitude of Mr. Lincoln seemed conciliatory. Most Southerners thought that a threat was conveyed in his statement that he would hold government property and collect taxes in the seceding States. Preparations for war and efforts to preserve peace were made simultaneously. There was talk of a constitutional amendment that would settle the slavery question. One day the indications were of early war; the next day the desire to save the precious union of the States appeared to prevail over extremes of bad counsel.

Every day, dark or hopeful, the eyes of all who loved their country were turned to Charleston, South Carolina. When the Palmetto had seceded, two of the forts in the lovely waters around that city had been occupied by Federal soldiers. Later, these troops, few in number, had been brought together in Fort Sumter, on an island in the harbor and within easy range of batteries constructed by the Carolinians. Secessionists contended that Sumter and all Federal public works must be under the control of the State. President Lincoln maintained that the forts were the property of the United States, that they would be supplied with food, and that they would be held by Federal troops. The critical question was whether, when supplies at Sumter ran low, Mr. Lincoln would send ships there to replenish stores. If he did, there was danger that South Carolina would fire on the ships and on the fort. That would be war.

Another condition watched with anxious concern was one created, in part, by the explosive situation at Charleston. The seceding States, which now numbered seven, had formed a separate government which they called the Confederate States of America. In this Confederacy were South Carolina, Mississippi, Florida, Alabama, Georgia, Louisiana and Texas, which had withdrawn from the Union in the order in which their names are listed. None of the so-called "border States," those closest to the North, had severed their old ties. Of these States, most powerful was Lee's own Virginia. Her General Assembly had called a convention which had assembled in Richmond before Lee's arrival in Washington, but this convention had been directed at the time of its election to submit to the approval of the voters any action it might take on secession. Two-thirds of the members of this convention were opposed to leaving the Federal Union, and were in favor of a policy of conciliation. At the same time, a majority of the convention were believed to be completely opposed to the coercion of the

States that had seceded. If the United States attacked the Confederacy, Virginia was almost certain to join in defence of the South. Because of this feeling, anyone could see that the action of Virginia might depend on events in Charleston Harbor.

Nobody watched those events with more anguish of spirit than did Colonel Lee. Few could have prayed more earnestly for peace or have felt more wrath against the noisy extremists on both sides who did not seem to realize that they had in their care the lives of tens of thousands of men and the continuance of a government that other thousands had died to establish and to preserve. Colonel Lee, as always, was for the preservation of the Union and was against secession, so long as his Mother State was a member of that Union and was not attacked and was not called upon to join in punishing other States. Consequently when he was promoted Colonel of the First Cavalry to take the place of Col. E. V. Sumner, who had been promoted to be Brigadier General, Lee did not hesitate to accept the commission. Virginia was still in the Union, where Lee hoped she could remain. If she could, he was as proud as ever to wear the uniform of the country.

Days passed. There was no change in the situation. Nor was there any moderation of the temper of angry men. The most discerning could not tell whether the tide was running toward war or was ebbing. Lee waited, hoped, held fast. Early in April there were hints that Sumter might be evacuated and the danger of conflict thereby reduced. Virginia's convention responded to this and to other omens of peace by two to one on April 4 against secession. The skies seemed brighter. Every honest heart felt relief. Then, suddenly, the black clouds of war rolled over the country. On the 7th of April, the Confederates cut off local fresh food from Sumter. Governor F. W. Pickens of South Carolina was informed by a messenger from President Lincoln that provisions would be sent to the fort by ship. The Southerners answered that if this were attempted, vessel and fort would be attacked. President Lincoln did not yield. On the 12th of April, 1861, one of the darkest days in American history, artillery fire was opened on Fort Sumter. Two days later, when the ramparts had been battered and the buildings had been set afire, the garrison surrendered. Not a life had been lost on either side, but passions had been inflamed beyond the power of reason or of prayer to restrain. President Lincoln on the 15th called on the States to furnish 75,000 troops "to suppress combinations" and to "cause the laws to be duly executed."

Virginia would be expected to furnish her part of the Army with which to punish the Southern States for seceding. This was the long-dreaded coercion that most Virginians inflexibly opposed. The convention in Richmond went into secret session on the 16th to decide what it would do. Next day, Colonel Lee at Arlington received an informal order to report to General Scott on the 18th. A message reached him the same day that Francis P. Blair, Sr., a prominent politician, would be glad if Lee called at the Blair home in Washington.

Lee went. He was ignorant of what the Virginia convention had done, if, indeed, it had taken any action, but he remained absolutely resolved in his own mind that if Virginia seceded, he would stand by her. In that spirit he waited. Mr. Blair explained that President Lincoln wished to know if Lee would accept command of the troops that were to be raised to restore Federal authority. Lee recorded later, in these simple words, his answer to Mr. Blair: "I declined the offer he made me to take command of the army that was to be brought into the field, stating as candidly and as courteously as I could, that though opposed to secession and deprecating war, I could take no part in an invasion of the Southern States."

From the Blair House, which still stands, Lee went to Scott's office and told him what happened. "Lee," the old General lamented, "you have made the greatest mistake of your life; but I feared it would be so." Scott continued in this strain, deeply distressed, and finally said, "If you propose to resign, it is proper that you should do so at once; your present attitude is equivocal." By that Scott meant that Lee might share councils a man should not enter if he did not intend to adhere to the cause that council represented. Then, too, Lee might receive orders he would not be willing to execute.

Lee had not thought of this. He had intended to stay as long as he properly could in the service he loved, and not to resign unless Virginia seceded. He would not be bound to resign his commission, in fact, until a possible ordinance of secession had been approved by the people of the State at a special election. Secession was not lawful before that.

Now that General Scott had raised a point of honor, Lee was acutely disturbed. He talked with his brother Smith and he wrestled alone with his problem. On the 19th he heard positively that the Virginia convention had voted to secede. That night he decided that he ought not to wait until the people passed on the action the convention had taken. He did not believe the war would wait on the election. His duty and his honor alike demanded that he resign immediately.

The next morning, April 20, he came downstairs at Arlington with two papers in his hand. "Well, Mary," he said, "the question is settled. Here is my letter of resignation and a letter I have written General Scott." Mrs. Lee understood and approved. She accurately stated the mind of the Colonel when she said, "My husband has wept tears of blood over this war, but as a man of honor and a Virginian, he must follow the destiny of his State."

The day after Lee wrote his resignation, which was dated April 20, he received a message that the Governor of Virginia, John Letcher, wished to see him in Richmond. On the 22nd Lee left Arlington, went to Richmond and during the evening waited on Mr. Letcher. The Governor, who had himself opposed secession, explained to Lee that the Virginia convention had authorized the appointment of a "commander of the military and naval forces of Virginia" under the direction of the Governor. The advisory council had recommended Lee: Would he accept?

It was a frightful responsibility but Virginia was in danger. Every loyal son had to defend her. Lee quietly replied that he would do his utmost. On the 23rd, the convention received him, and, through its President, announced that it approved the Governor's appointment. In a few sober words, Lee accepted: "I would have much preferred had your choice fallen on an abler man. Trusting in Almighty God, an approving conscience, and the aid of my fellow-citizens, I devote myself to the service of my native State, in whose behalf alone will I ever again draw my sword."

CHAPTER SEVEN

Ten Months Without a Battle

A BEWILDERING new world seemed to have been created by secession. Familiar old rivers, such as the Potomac and the Ohio, became foreign frontiers. Life-long friends were made enemies overnight. Hideous war was coming to those who had lived together in peace for eighty years. The division was not so much within the States as it was between the States.

This war would be different from the Revolution and more terrible in another respect: It would be a war of the fastest movement in history. Troops could move five times as rapidly as in 1781. Still again, Lee's hero, General Washington, had been compelled to rely on slow ships or on mounted messengers who took weeks to carry a dispatch from New York or Philadelphia to Charleston, South Carolina. Now a commander could send a telegram and get an answer in an hour or two.

The sections that fought this new war of swift movement would not be equally matched. In wealth, in manufactures and in total population, the North was by far the more powerful, but the young men of the Confederacy were more accustomed to out-of-door life than many of the Northerners were. Nearly all Southerners believed they could beat the Union with the odds two to one against them.

General Lee—now General for the first time—did not deceive himself. He knew the resources of the North and he did not underrate its courage or its character. His first prayer was that God would spare

America the curse of sectional war. "I should like, above all things," he wrote, "that our difficulties might be peaceably arranged, and still trust that a merciful God, whom I know will not unnecessarily afflict us, may yet allay the fury for war." Often he said, "In God alone must be our trust."

Next to the help of the Almighty, Lee wanted three things for the conflict—time to prepare, weapons to use, understanding on the part of the people that the frightful ordeal before them would call for utmost sacrifice. Soldiers by thousands were volunteering and were clamoring for more and better firearms than Virginia could provide. Every day brought nearer the time when the Northern army would invade the State. Lee and a few other trained men labored almost frantically to prepare for the shock, but they found a majority of the people, from wisest to weakest, convinced that the one battle would end the war. The Southern victory would be overwhelming. Peace and independence would come within ninety days. That was the talk everywhere. Lee could not make speeches or write newspaper articles to rid the people of this illusion, but when he had opportunity he spoke plainly. One day a father with little brains but much pride in his five-year-old child brought the boy to Lee's office and insisted on a personal interview because, he said, the little boy wanted to give the General a Bible. When admitted, the man had the boy present the book and then he said: "What is General Lee going to do to General Scott?"

The youngster, who had been well coached, answered, "He is going to whip him out of his breeches."

The father thought that was tremendously cute, but the General stiffened. He stood the boy in front of him and spoke squarely over the little fellow's shoulders at the father: "My dear little boy, you should not use such expressions. War is a serious matter, and General

Scott is a great and good soldier. None of us can tell what the result of the contest will be."

The proud father went on his way; Lee returned to work for which there never seemed to be hours enough, even when he was not interrupted needlessly. After he had done all he could in so brief a time to prepare Virginia for defence, the State formally ratified the ordinance of secession and linked her fate with that of the South. Lee became a Confederate General. His chief duties for the time were to assist Jefferson Davis, the President of the Confederacy, which moved its capital from Montgomery, Alabama, to Richmond.

Soon after Lee undertook these new duties, a small Confederate force defeated a Federal column at a place named Big Bethel, not far from Lee's old station at Fortress Monroe. This victory on the 10th of June led every braggart to say "I told you so!" The next month, on Bull Run, in Virginia, about twenty-five miles South of Washington, another and a much more costly defeat was inflicted on a large Union army by Confederate troops under Lee's old chum, Joseph E. Johnston, and his fellow-engineer of the Mexican War, P. G. T. Beauregard. The beaten Federals ran back almost to Washington that 21st day of July. So complete seemed their defeat that many Confederates thought the war had been won. They did not believe it would be necessary to get arms and to make any other preparations for another campaign.

In Western Virginia, about the same time, events of a different sort were occurring. A strong Federal column had marched down from the Baltimore and Ohio Railroad and had beaten a few thousand Confederates near Rich Mountain. The Confederate General, Robert S. Garnett, had been killed. There was danger that the Federals might advance to Staunton, Virginia, the principal city of the rich Shenandoah Valley, which fed many mouths. The loss of Staunton and of the

Valley must be prevented. Lee, said President Davis, must go to Western Virginia and stop the Federals.

Small chance there was, in Lee's opinion, of winning a victory in that difficult region but he hastened to Staunton by railway and proceeded from that town on horseback to Monterey and on into the Alleghany Mountains. Few mountains are like them, so overpowering and yet so intimate. Lee observed and delighted in all the splendors of the Alleghenies. "What a glorious world Almighty God has given us," Lee reflected; "how thankless and ungrateful we are, and how we labour to mar his gifts."

On the long ridge known as Cheat Mountain Lee found the Federals. They were well located and they could not be forced from their position otherwise than by hard, secret marches over obscure trails. Lee soon discovered that he had even more difficult things to do than that of getting in rear of Cheat Mountain. He had, first of all, to cope with much sickness on the part of the soldiers. Some of them did not know how to take care of themselves physically. Others had come from remote farms where they never had been exposed to the common diseases of childhood. Measles had broken out among the troops and had caused the sickness of thousands and the death of scores.

The second condition that hampered Lee was bad weather. Rain fell almost all the time. One soldier wrote: "In all my experience of the war I never saw as much mud. It seemed to rain every day and it got to be a saying in our company that you must not halloo loud, for if you should we would immediately have a hard shower, and when some of the men on their return from picket had to shoot their guns off to get the load out, it brought on a regular flood. Granville Gray always said it rained *thirty-two* days in August . . . I saw dead mules lying in the road, with nothing but their ears showing above the mud."

Worse than mud or measles was the unconcealed jealousy of the General in charge of the troops that faced Cheat Mountain. This officer, W. W. Loring, was a younger man than Lee but he had been an active Indian fighter when Lee was a staff officer and he resented the coming of Lee into the country he was defending.

Besides sickness and bad weather and the jealousy of Loring, there was a lack of discipline on the part of the inexperienced soldiers. They were willing to do anything they knew how to do but they knew little to do. This irritated some officers who were "very military" in manner, but it prompted General Lee to apply a rule he long previously had made a part of his code, the rule of treating every man, even the humblest, as a human being and not as a mere cog in a machine. He always would listen to every soldier who came to ask a question or to make a complaint. Once, at least, in dealing with green soldiers in Western Virginia he had an experience that made him smile, though a man of different temper might have sworn. While Lee was examining with his field-glasses a position where he thought the enemy might be, a private came up to him and waited expectantly. Lee took his glasses from his eyes and asked what he could do for the man. Without a single touch of embarrassment, the soldier explained that he was "out of tobacco": could the General let him have a chew? As Lee neither smoked nor chewed, he could not oblige the soldier but he had a tobacco-loving staff officer supply the fighting man's need as if that were part of the regular duty of officers. This sort of courtesy was one of the things that made Lee's soldiers like him from the first and soon love him.

By courtesy, by diligence, by making the best of adverse conditions, Lee improved everything, even the jealous temper of General Loring, but all this took time. It was the second week in September, 1861, before Lee could perfect a plan for getting in rear of Cheat

Mountain. He arranged that part of his men were to attack in front while others who had climbed painfully over the ridges were to cut off the retreat of the Federals. The plan was excellent, but the men who undertook to carry it out, September 11–12, did not know enough about marching and fighting to do what was required for success. The attack failed completely. Lee had to move back and had to give up hope of doing anything more than preventing a farther advance by the Union soldiers. This was, in Lee's own words a "grievous disappointment" to him, but he assumed the blame for the failure. He would not tell even the President what had happened until he exacted from Mr. Davis a promise that nothing would be said or done about the failure of those who had not been able to carry out his order.

From Cheat Mountain, Lee had to proceed to the valley of the Kanawha River, about eighty miles to the southwest. A Federal army was threatening an advance up the Kanawha. To oppose this army were two small Confederate forces under the command of Brig. Henry A. Wise and Brig. Gen. John B. Floyd. These men had received no professional training as soldiers. They had been politicians before the war and, though both were patriotic, they had been unable to bury their rivalries for their country's sake. Between them, so much ill will and jealousy developed that they expended much of their energies in writing angry letters to one another, or to the President or to General Lee.

When Lee arrived at Meadow Bluff on the 21st of September, 1861, relations between Wise and Floyd were at the breaking point. The two occupied separate positions; neither was willing to yield his ground. Lee worked to reconcile them and finally had their troops almost ready to meet the enemy's assault. Then, one night, the Federals withdrew. Another failure was charged against Lee. When he was asked why he had not attacked or pursued, he explained that he did not have food for his army. The gentleman who asked the question was not satisfied. "Your reputation was suffering," he said, "the press was denouncing you, your own state was losing confidence in you, and the army needed a victory to add to its enthusiasm." Lee shook his head. "I could not afford," he replied, "to sacrifice the lives of five or six hundred of my people to silence public clamor."

In that spirit, Lee left the valley of the Kanawha on the 30th of October and returned to Richmond. His reception by the public and by the newspapers was cool. It was said that he was too much of a "'theoretical soldier." The campaign, asserted one critic, "was conducted by a general who had never fought a battle, who had a pious horror of guerillas, and whose extreme tenderness of blood induced him to depend exclusively upon the resources of strategy to essay the achievement of victory without the cost of life."

President Davis was not of this mind. On August 31, at his instance, Congress had made Lee a full General, the highest rank in Confederate service. The President knew the character of Lee and had faith in his ability. Almost as soon as General Lee reached Richmond and reported, the President ordered him to proceed to the coast of South Carolina, where the Federals had assembled a large fleet. Lee was to meet and to defeat the troops who might be put ashore from the transport the warships escorted.

This proved a task of no great difficulty. The Federal commander was slow and cautious, but the work of preparing the defence of the Savannah River and of improving the forts around Charleston had to be performed in the face of laziness of some and the apparent indifference of others. Some of this was amusing. Lee, for instance, greatly loved horses and, on his rounds, occasionally would stop at army stables and examine the animals. One day, as he was leaving, he saw a hostler look at him hard and then heard the man inquire of a companion: "I say, Sergeant, who is that durned old fool? He's always a-pokin' around my hosses as if he meant to steal one of 'em."

Not all those who were suspicious of the new commander were persons who knew no better. Brig. Gen. R. S. Ripley, who had married a Charleston lady of distinguished family, took an acute dislike of General Lee and belittled him in every possible way. Lee ignored this criticism, if he knew of it, and worked with right-minded men until the coast was fairly secure and the port of Charleston was stronger than ever. The sun of confidence continued to shine there, but elsewhere the outlook grew darker daily. Two of the most important defences in Tennessee, Fort Henry and Fort Donelson, were captured by the Federals in February. Union troops landed about the same time on Roanoke Island, North Carolina, and overwhelmed a small Confederate force near the place where Sir Walter Raleigh had established the "lost colony." Lee met this bad news with his usual courage. He wrote: "We must make up our minds to meet with reverses and to overcome them. I hope God will at last crown our efforts with success. But the contest must be long and severe, and the whole country must go through much suffering. It is necessary we should be humbled and taught to be less boastful, less selfish and more devoted to right and justice to all the world."

This was written on the 8th of February, 1862, the very day of the disaster at Roanoke Island. After that, for three weeks, there were many evidences of Federal preparations for a Federal naval attack on the Savannah River, but no battle was fought. In fact, the 23rd of February ended for Lee ten months of Confederate service in which he had not fought a single battle. It was a period of training, a period of becoming acquainted with the men he was to lead, a period that ended dramatically on the 2nd of March with a request from the President that he come to Richmond.

CHAPTER EIGHT

Seven Armies Face a Fight

UPON HIS RETURN to Richmond early in March, 1862, General Lee found a desperate situation. Government armories were almost empty of powder. Thousands of soldiers who had promised to serve one year were nearing the end of that term and acted as if they did not intend to enlist again. Some of the people who had been boastful and overconfident in 1861 were in a panic of despair. They said President Davis was making so many mistakes that the war would certainly be lost unless some competent General took charge of the armies. Mr. Davis, a sensitive man, resented this. He had confidence in himself and intended to be what the constitution of the Confederacy said the President was to be, commander-in-chief of the army and of the navy.

Lee at once became unwillingly involved in the quarrel. Congressmen who wanted an experienced commanding General did not all agree that Lee was the ideal man for the place, but they knew the President had faith in him and they were willing to accept him. A compromise was reached. Davis vetoed a bill that established the position of commanding General, but on the 13th of March he named Lee to conduct under his direction the military operations of the Confederate armies. This order did not give Lee clearly-stated duties and it did what no order ever should do: It put on him responsibility without giving him power. Lee realized this and did not like the assignment. "It will give me great pleasure," he said, "to do anything

I can to relieve (the President) and serve the country, but I cannot see either advantage or pleasure in my duties."

In spite of this feeling, General Lee was as solidly determined to do his best as he had been when he was a cadet at West Point. As often happens, opportunity developed from honest willingness to study and to work for success. Slowly at first and then more and more rapidly, Lee and some of the other Confederate leaders worked out a remarkable plan. To this day, long after the death of all the Confederate Generals, foreign soldiers come to the South to study what Lee and the others did in the spring of 1862.

It is too long and complicated a story to be told here, but some parts of it were thrilling. The great Union Army of the Potomac was the largest and best equipped that ever had been assembled at that time in America. This host of about 100,000 men was under Maj. Gen. George B. McClellan, who had been one of the youngest of the engineers with Lee in the Mexican War. McClellan moved his immense army by vessel to Hampton Roads, where the James River enters Chesapeake Bay. Then McClellan marched toward Richmond up the peninsula between the James and the York. The Confederates opposed him with nearly all the troops that had been in Northern Virginia under Lee's old friend Gen. Joseph E. Johnston. He was an able leader; his soldiers were willing to fight. The trouble was, they were outnumbered.

Besides, the Confederates learned that many other Union troops were gathering at Fredericksburg, slightly more than fifty miles North of Richmond. These troops were known as McDowell's Army. They might march down at any time in May, join McClellan and share in the capture of the Confederate capital.

Johnston's Army, in other words, might have been considered a good-sized boy who was looking to the East and was facing a much larger boy, McClellan's Army. While Johnston was trying to hold his own against McClellan, there was danger that McDowell might creep up on the left and make the fight two to one against Johnston.

The Confederates had, also, a small army in the wide and lovely Shenandoah Valley, which lies between the Blue Ridge and the Allegheny Mountains. This little army was under the same Thomas Jonathan Jackson who was seen in the pedregal during the Mexican War. Jackson had resigned from the army in 1852 and had become a professor at the Virginia Military Institute. He had been a dull teacher, but after the war opened, he soon had become distinguished. In the First Battle of Manassas he had stood so firmly that another Confederate commander had said he was a "Stonewall." That name stuck, though the soldiers called him "Old Jack." He did not have in May, 1862, sufficient troops to keep McDowell from moving to join McClellan in beating Johnston. In fact, "Stonewall" Jackson faced three Federal Armies in Western Virginia, under Gen. N. P. Banks, Gen. R. H. Milroy, and the famous explorer, Gen. John C. Frémont.

The picture, then, might be likened to a fight in which seven boys were engaged. Johnston was sparring with McClellan while McDowell was rolling up his sleeves to come down on Johnston's left and join in beating the Confederate. Jackson was smaller than any of this trio, was behind Johnston, and was facing North in the expectation of a fight with Milroy, Banks and Frémont, each of whom was about his size.

What was Lee, as the President's adviser, to recommend that these Confederates do? Whatever Lee urged, he might get into trouble, because Johnston, who had a hot temper, might get jealous of Lee's "interference" with Jackson or with him. In theory, Jackson was under Johnston, even if Johnston was too busy with his own fight to give much attention to Jackson.

As tactfully as Lee could, he corresponded with Jackson and with Johnston and finally concluded that it would be possible to save the situation in this way: The three Generals who were facing Jackson were not close together. If Jackson, a fine fighter, could beat Milroy and Banks and Frémont one after another, then Jackson might scare McDowell so badly that the Federal would be slow about joining McClellan. While McDowell waited, Johnston might find a chance to hit McClellan to knock him out.

This was a daring plan. Its prospect of success depended almost entirely on Jackson's speed and hard hitting. He must "take on" the three Federals in Western Virginia, before the other part of the plan could be undertaken. Jackson was willing. Some of his officers called him a religious fanatic, and others thought him crazy, but he amazed them all. Early in May he attacked Milroy, who fought hard and then ran away. Jackson hurried back to the Shenandoah Valley and suddenly hit Banks from the left at Front Royal, while the Union commander was not expecting a fight. Banks hurled around to meet the Confederates, but when he started moving northward, he found the lower Shenandoah Valley like a bowling alley. Once he began rolling he had to "keep going." Jackson hit him again and drove him across the Potomac (First Battle of Winchester, May 25, 1862).

When Jackson hastened in pursuit of Banks's Army, Lee lost touch with "Stonewall." Nobody knew in Richmond exactly what success Jackson was having. Everyone was waiting for Johnston to attack McClellan and was wondering whether Johnston could do this before McDowell joined McClellan. On the 27th of May the long-awaited bad news was received: McDowell was marching southward! Johnston did not tell Davis or even Lee what he intended to do, but it appeared that he had to strike at once or face both McClellan and McDowell.

Then, on the 29th, equally-startling news reached the Confederates.

McDowell had turned back! He was not coming to Richmond, at least not then. It seemed a mystery and almost a miracle but the reason was Jackson. His defeat of Milroy and then of Banks had created alarm for the safety of McDowell's rear and of the city of Washington. Two days before McDowell started his march, he had begun to send troops to stop Jackson. The move on the 27th had not been an actual advance but an effort to find out how many Confederates were in front of him.

The halt of McDowell gave Johnston a chance to attack McClellan at a place known as Seven Pines or Fair Oaks about seven miles East of Richmond. Johnston struck when he did, May 31, because he believed high water would divide the Federals in such a way that the odds against them would not be heavy. He was mistaken in this. The battle was a bloody draw. While it was nearing its close, General Johnston was badly wounded. It was manifest he would be out of the fighting for months.

That evening as Lee was riding with Davis from the battlefield to Richmond, the President directed him to take command of the Army the next day. All the opportunities, all the responsibilities now were combined. Lee must save Richmond or fail hopelessly and forever as a soldier.

CHAPTER NINE

Lee Fails to Get Team Work

BEFORE LEE could reach the field on the 1st of June, 1862, the Battle of Seven Pines was renewed and then was ended without victory on either side. Soon the Generals moved the armies back to about the ground the troops had held before the bloody action had opened. These tired senior officers were not enthusiastic in their welcome of their new commander. Most of them knew Lee and respected him as a man but they regarded him not as a fighter but as an engineer. He might be "too theoretical," some of the Generals thought, to be a successful leader in the field. Besides, the men at the head of the Army were somewhat like the members of a club. They might quarrel among themselves and might not like one another, but they would stand together against an outsider. In the eyes of some of them Lee was just that—an "outsider."

For his own part, Lee seldom talked about other persons, and then always in an effort to be fair to them. He had learned during thirty-seven years as cadet and as soldier to accept men as they were and to make the best of their abilities by appealing to their higher impulses. Had he been more critical, he might have marvelled and perhaps have laughed grimly at the strange differences in the men who led the diverse units of the army. A regiment was supposed to include ten companies of 100 men each. Four regiments made a Brigade, which would be under a Brigadier General. When four Brigades were put together they constituted a Division, which in theory consisted of

16,000 but seldom really numbered more than half that number. Usually a Division was commanded by a Major General. In the Army that Lee received from Johnston there were nine Major Generals. Several of these were patriotic men of no great ability, but some of the division commanders were interesting and capable. "Stonewall" Jackson, still in the Shenandoah Valley, was the best known of them. Next to him in soldierly qualities, though not yet widely known was a native South Carolinian, aged 41, James Longstreet by name. He was of middle height, somewhat heavy and slightly deaf. Before the war he had been in the paymasters department and in 1861 he had the reputation of living gaily, but the following winter he lost three of his children during a single week in an epidemic of scarlet fever. After that he was a reserved, often a silent man.

Ranking with Longstreet was Maj. Gen. John B. Magruder, about six feet three inches tall, magnificent in dress and in manner, who spoke with a curious lisp and always rode at a gallop. Still another well-known Major General was Daniel H. Hill of North Carolina, age 41, a man of high character but somewhat disposed to be over-critical, as sharp tongued as he was sharp witted. The youngest of the Major Generals was Ambrose Powell Hill, a Virginian in his 37th year. He was a thin man of average height and of somewhat unstable health.

Lee did not have much time to study these men because the Federal Army was almost at the gates of Richmond. Union outposts at one point were so close to the city that they could tell the time by the chiming of the bells in Richmond towers. McClellan had more and better cannon, as well as more infantry, than Lee commanded. If given time, the Federals could blast their way into the Confederate capital. Lee had to hold them off until he was strong enough to attack them and to drive them from in front of Richmond.

The one way to keep these tens of thousands of bluecoats at a distance was to build fortifications they could not easily capture or blow to pieces with artillery. Lee undertook at once to have these earthworks built but he encountered much resistance on the part of the soldiers, the very men whom he was trying to protect. They grumbled that he was the "King of Spades," not a fighting General. Digging dirt, they said, was no work for gentlemen. Lee persisted. "There is," he wrote, "nothing so military as labor, and nothing so important to an army as to save the lives of its soldiers." Fortunately for Lee, during the very first weeks of his command, the weather was rainy. Much of the flat country around Richmond became a mire. The Federals could not advance their heavy guns or move their troops quickly. Lee consequently was able to meet the first requirement of holding the enemy.

The second task of Lee was that of getting sufficient troops to attack McClellan. Almost all the Armies of the Confederacy were facing larger numbers of Federals somewhere in the South. There were no unused troops or reserves. To get men for Richmond, Lee had to take them from somewhere else. In this, the knowledge he had gained as a young engineer on Cockspur Island helped him. He knew that when summer came on the coast of Georgia and of South Carolina, the Federal troops could not remain close to the swamps. The Unionists would have to withdraw because of malaria. When they did, the Confederates who opposed them might come temporarily to Richmond and join in an attack on McClellan.

Lee's second hope of getting more troops was through Jackson. After "Stonewall" had driven Banks across the Potomac in May, Frémont's Army and troops from McDowell had tried to cut off the Confederates. Jackson had been forced to retreat at top speed southward up the Valley. He had been able to get away, though by a narrow margin. Then, on successive days (June 8 and 9, 1862) he had beaten Frémont and then McDowell's men under Gen. James Shields. This left Jackson free for a time. Lee hoped that he could help Jackson invade the North, or at least make the Federals think Jackson was going to do that. Then Jackson might come quickly to Richmond, help Lee defeat McClellan and get back to the Valley before the Federals could do much mischief. To return to the comparison of the boys who were fighting, Jackson would run down, help the medium-sized Lee (Johnston) beat the big McClellan and hurry back to his own street to deal with those who might gang up on him.

McClellan's Army was in a curious position. The next year, President Lincoln cautioned one of his Generals not to "take any risk of being entangled upon the river, like an ox jumped half over a fence and liable to be torn by dogs front and rear without a fair chance to gore one way or kick the other." McClellan was in exactly that situation when Lee decided to attack him across a little river that has the musical Indian name Chickahominy. McClellan was astride this watercourse for two reasons. First, he had put one wing of his army North of the Chickahominy to join with McDowell in May. Second, McClellan was getting all the food for his Army and all his supplies from a place called the White House, on the Pamunkey River. General McClellan had told himself that if he did not keep troops on the north side of the river, Lee would go down that bank and destroy the railroad. Then McClellan would have to starve or retreat. He had to protect what soldiers call the lines of supply.

Lee decided to make the most of the fact that McClellan was "like an ox jumped half over" the Chickahominy. The Confederate commander was not sure the Federals were getting *all* their supplies "by rail." He thought they might be sending some of their food and fodder by wagons and might be guarding the road as well as the railway. To be certain about this, Lee decided to send out cavalry on a reconnaissance. To lead this cavalry he selected the chief of his mounted troops, a young man of 29 who soon was to become one of Lee's most famous soldiers—Brig. Gen. James Ewell Brown Stuart. Because Stuart's initials spell "Jeb," he always went by that nickname in the army. At West Point he had been called "Beauty" Stuart, because he had a receding chin that gave him a very ugly profile. This was now concealed under a beard that would have suited a brigand in an opera.

On June 13–14, with about 1,400 companions, Stuart rode entirely around McClellan's Army. By the morning of the 14th, he was on the flooded banks of the lower Chickahominy, far from all help by Lee. The Federals were pursuing. It looked as if Stuart and all his companions would be captured, but "Jeb's" men built a crude bridge and got across the river just before the first of the Federals galloped up to the bank of the stream. Afterward, one of Stuart's friends remarked: "That was a tight place at the river, General. If the enemy had come down on us, you would have been compelled to have surrendered."

"No," Stuart answered, "one other course was left."

"What was that?"

"To die game."

The information the courageous Stuart brought back was most useful. It confirmed Lee's belief that "the ox on the fence" could be "torn" in front and worried in rear. Jackson's "pack" was to come by train as quickly and secretly as possible from the Shenandoah Valley and was to march down the north side of the Chickahominy and attack the flank of McClellan. Other troops were to be ready to help. Still others were to remain on the south side of the Chickahominy and were to beat off any attack the enemy might make there.

Jackson began to move his Army from the Shenandoah Valley on the

18th of June, and by the 23rd he had his troops so well advanced that he took horse at Frederick's Hall and rode to Lee's headquarters, where the other Generals who were to share in the attack had been invited to meet. The first any of them knew of Jackson's approach was when "Stonewall's" brother-in-law rode up and saw him leaning over the fence. Jackson was tired then, but after everything had been arranged at the conference, he insisted on riding back that night to rejoin his troops. He did not realize it, but by remaining two nights in the saddle, he was wearing himself out before the battle opened and the heaviest strain began.

The 26th of June, the day set for the attack, opened with intense excitement and clear, fine weather. Everything seemed in order for the first major battle by the new commander of the army, the battle on which the fate of Richmond and even of the Confederacy might depend.

Lee rode out early to an advanced battery from which he could watch the valley of the Chickahominy down which Jackson was to move. Hours passed without a message from Jackson, or a sound of his approach, or the appearance of a single gray-coated Confederate north of the Chickahominy. Something had gone wrong; Lee did not know what. At last, about 3 o'clock in the afternoon, A. P. Hill lost patience and decided to push across the river without waiting longer for Jackson.

The excellent soldiers of Hill were as impatient as he was. Once they reached the opposite side of the Chickahominy, they turned downstream and soon found the enemy near the village of Mechanicsville. A confused and costly attack followed. A. P. Hill did not know that the open field in front of him dropped abruptly to a deep ravine in which there were a creek and a mill-race. When Hill's men rushed forward, they ran down into this ravine and came under a heavy fire from artillerymen and infantry on the high ground across the stream. Fifteen hundred Confederates were killed or wounded. Nothing whatever was heard of Jackson.

On June 27, the morning after this Battle of Mechanicsville or Beaver Dam Creek, A. P. Hill found that the Federals were leaving the stream and were moving down the north bank of the river. The Confederates thought this retreat must have been made because the Federals had found out that Jackson was approaching. Nothing positive was known until Lee reached Walnut Grove Church, which is about a mile East of the creek where the battle of the 26th had been fought. In front of the church a tall man in a dust-covered gray uniform was awaiting Lee. The hair of this newcomer was a chestnut brown and had a slight curl. His heavy beard, which was almost square, was of the same color. His nose was aquiline. His brow was not visible under the cap that shielded his weak blue eyes, but it was broad and high. When he spoke to Lee, it was in a low, half-muffled voice.

Such was the first sight many officers had of "Stonewall" Jackson, who was at that time the most admired soldier of the South. Jackson did not explain, nor did Lee ask why the troops from the Shenandoah Valley had been late on the 26th. Like every wise man, Lee talked of what could be done on the new day, not of what had been left undone the previous day. The enemy was in retreat down the Chickahominy and doubtless would take a new position and offer battle again: Jackson must hasten with his troops to a place called Cold Harbor, which the Federals would have to pass if they tried to hold their railroad to the White House.

Jackson rode off; Lee continued with the troops of A. P. Hill. After another two miles, the head of the column reached a hill that overlooked a little stream on which stood a grist mill—Gaines' Mill it was called. For a few minutes there seemed to be a chance that a battle would be fought for this crossing, but the enemy hurried off. Hill's men followed and soon came to thick woodland that led down through a dense tangle of undergrowth to another stream, known as Boatswain's Swamp. Behind this, on a long, strong ridge that faced North, the Federals were drawn up and were ready to pour a terrific fire into the Confederates. Hill attacked at once and with fury but he could not get his men across the swamp. Lee watched anxiously as one small assault after another failed. Although Lee had more men near at hand than the enemy did, it seemed impossible to get the Southern troops to act as a unit in those confusing woods.

Finally Jackson came in sight. He was more nearly covered with dust than he had been at the church and he was sucking steadily at a lemon. After an exchange of greetings, Lee remarked, "That fire is very heavy; do you think your men can stand it?"

Jackson listened and then replied tersely: "They can stand almost anything; they can stand that."

Even after Jackson threw his men into the struggle, hundreds were wounded before the Army began to fight as a single machine. About dusk, the different divisions seemed to mesh into gear. The first breakthrough was made on the right of Hill's line by a superb Brigade, chiefly of Texans, under the command of Brig. Gen. John B. Hood, the same Hood whom Lee had cautioned years before against a foolish marriage.

This Battle of Gaines' Mill ended at nightfall. The Union army was forced to retreat; it was not destroyed. Lee's first victory had been won but it had been bought by some of the best blood of the South. Not less than 8,000 had been killed or wounded. The Federals had suffered heavily, too, and had lost many fine cannon and hundreds of prisoners.

The next morning, June 28, while the dead were being buried and the wounded were being carried to the rear, General Lee went in search of his youngest son, Robert, who was a private in a battery already famous, the Rockbridge Artillery. Robert himself best described what happened: "Most of the men were lying down, many sleeping, myself among the latter number. To get some shade and to be out of the way, I had crawled under a caisson, and was busy making up many lost hours of rest. Suddenly I was rudely awakened by a comrade, prodding me with a sponge-staff as I had failed to be aroused by his call, and was told to get up and come out, as someone wished to see me. Half awake, I staggered out, and found myself face to face with General Lee and his staff. Their fresh uniforms, bright equipments and well-groomed horses contrasted so forcibly with the war-worn appearance of our command that I was completely dazed. It took me a moment or two to realize what it all meant, but when I saw my father's loving eyes and smile it became clear to me that he had ridden out to see if I was safe and to ask how I was getting along. I remember well how curiously those with him gazed at me, and I am sure it must have struck them as very odd that such a dirty, ragged, unkempt youth could have been the son of this grand-looking victorious commander."

By this time, Lee had learned that all the Federals had left the north bank of the Chickahominy, but he did not know more than that till afternoon. Then he and his companions saw a strange sight. South of them, across the river, a cloud appeared. It rose from the ground, instead of descending from the sky. It was dust, not mist, and it was moving, moving toward the East. Everyone made the same remark: The dust came from men's feet, from horses' hoofs and from wagon wheels. McClellan was in retreat from Richmond! He might be going eastward to get back across the Chickahominy to the White House or he might be heading for James River, which was about ten miles to the South. In either event, the Confederates must pursue swiftly and, if possible, must catch McClellan while he was on the move. He then could be torn to pieces.

For three successive days Lee tried to do this. On the 29th at Savage Station, on the 30th at Glendale or White Oak Swamp, and again on the 1st of July at Malvern Hill, the Confederates sought to overwhelm the Army of the Potomac. Each time, when the day's fight ended, the Federals left the battlefield and took a new position, but in none of the contests was Lee able to get his entire army into action at the same moment. A part of the army, rather than the whole of it, had to make the attacks. The soldiers fought magnificently but they simply were not strong enough, at the decisive moment, to put into their attack the punch necessary to destroy the Unionists.

It so happened that one of the Federal Brigades that struggled hardest to beat off the Southern attacks was commanded by Brig. Gen. Abner Doubleday. Few of the Confederates ever had heard of him then. Probably none of the Southerners knew that Doubleday as a young man had persuaded his friends to change the rules of town ball or "three-hole cat" and had made a new game, which was to be called baseball. Even if the Confederates had realized that they were fighting the inventor of the future national game they would have been too busy in those desperate battles to think about sport. Afterward, if Lee and his lieutenants had reflected, they would have said that they failed of complete success because they lacked what Doubleday's game required—perfect teamwork. There were too many individual stars among the Confederate leaders. Some of them seemed to be more concerned about their reputation for fine plays than about the success of the team. Others let small obstacles discourage them. A few were so painstakingly slow that they never got to the battleground till the fighting was over.

In spite of this, the Battles of the Seven Days, as they were called, everywhere were hailed as a great Confederate victory. When the Southern offensive began, McClellan was within five miles of Richmond. At the close of the campaign, he was hemmed in a camp 18 miles from the city. Under the guns of warships in James River, he was secure from attack but he was himself unable at the time to assail the capital again. He had lost fifty-two field guns, 31,000 small arms and about 10,000 prisoners. His total "casualties," that is, his killed, wounded and prisoners, numbered 15,849 in an army of 105,000. None of Lee's artillery and few of his soldiers had fallen into the hands of the enemy, but total Confederate casualties were 20,141 of a gross strength of 85,500. In other words, Lee had lost a larger percentage of his troops than McClellan had. Richmond had been saved but the price had been grievous.

The Confederate people saw the victory and did not count the cost. At a time when the abandonment of the capital and even the defeat of the Southern cause had seemed probable, Lee had triumphed over the enemy and had changed the whole outlook. Some of those who had been most violent in denouncing his failure in Western Virginia acclaimed him now. The soldiers ceased to grumble about the "King of Spades." They appreciated his leadership in battle and they knew also, how he had improved their rations, their equipment and their medical care.

Lee himself was of all Southerners the one least excited over the outcome of the battles for Richmond. He was grateful to God and to his army, but he felt that McClellan should have been destroyed. In his report, Lee said that one reason for failure to achieve complete success was inability to discover quickly what the Federals were doing in a wooded country of a bewildering number of narrow, bad roads. Lee might have added in perfect truth that the slowness of some Generals and the excitability or inexperience of others had been responsible in part for the fatal lack of teamwork.

How was Lee to deal with these men? One way, of course, was to put the blame squarely on them in his report and then to try them before a court martial or to dismiss them from the army. By doing this, Lee might have put the fear of God in the heart of other careless officers and he might have convinced the South that if he had received better assistance he would have won an overwhelming victory. Lee did not even consider this stern course. In his report he dealt as considerately as possible with the incompetent leaders, and, meantime, he quietly and quickly had them assigned to duties that suited them better.

The case of "Stonewall" Jackson was different. He had not arrived in time to do his part in the opening battle. On the 30th, Jackson had failed to cross White Oak Swamp and to attack the rear of the Federals when many officers had 'thought he could have done so. In others words, the great Jackson had come to Richmond with a reputation and a popularity much above that of Lee, but it might have been alleged that he had let Lee down in a supreme crisis. If Lee had been a jealous man, he could have dwelt on Jackson's shortcomings and probably could have destroyed Jackson as a rival. Instead of doing this, Lee placed no direct blame on Jackson in his report and did not even inquire what actually had happened. Lee went to his death, eight years later, in ignorance of the reasons for Jackson's delay on June 30. The explanation involved many things. Chief among them, probably, was excess of zeal rather than lack of it. Jackson was so determined to do his full duty that he lost sleep upon which he was exceptionally dependent. He was benumbed mentally on the days when he held the key to victory.

Lee, to repeat, did not know this, but he knew a soldier when he saw one and he had the instincts of a generous soul in dealing with the patriot who had won shining victories in the Valley. Although Lee never said so in plain words, he evidently believed that all Jackson needed to demonstrate his full capacities was another chance.

A chance for some able Confederate leader was developing in Northern Virginia. Parts of McDowell's scattered Army and the fragments of the defeated troops of Banks and Frémont had been placed under Maj. Gen. John Pope, a self-confident officer who had achieved some success in the Mississippi Valley. This large force had been named the Army of Virginia and it was being concentrated on the railroad that led through the very center of the State. Pope's Army must be met and defeated. The only way of doing this was to take troops from in front of Richmond. As soon as Lee reached this conclusion, he decided to send Jackson. How well Jackson repaid this confidence, the events of the next two months were to show.

CHAPTER TEN

A Desperate Race Ends in Victory

WHEN JACKSON left the Richmond front on the 13th of July, 1862, to meet Pope's Army of Virginia, the situation was similar in some ways to that which had existed when seven boys had been ready to fight in May. The boys, that is, the armies, were larger though not quite so numerous. Lee, taking Johnston's place, was watching McClellan who was sore but still strong in a position from which he could not make a heavy swing at Lee. In Central Virginia was John Pope, powerful and arrogant. Facing him was the smaller Army of Jackson. At Fredericksburg was a boy of unknown size, who turned out to be Rufus King. He was expected to join Pope in trying to beat Jackson. Besides these five—Lee and McClellan, Jackson and Pope and King—another boy was coming into the fight. He was Ambrose Burnside, who had done well in North Carolina and had moved by ship to Hampton Roads. There he and his men were waiting aboard their transports to steam to some unknown destination. If Burnside helped McClellan, the Army of the Potomac would be as strong as it had been prior to the Seven Days. Lee would have to take on both Burnside and McClellan. On the other hand, if Burnside reenforced Pope, the Army of Virginia would outnumber Jackson so heavily that "Stonewall" must be given more troops.

The prospect of this six-cornered fight was enough to alarm any man who did not have faith in his army. Lee had that faith but he saw two things clearly: He had to get better teamwork than the army had shown during the Seven Days, and he had to prepare for a race as well as for a fight. The signal for the race would be the departure of Burnside for Northern Virginia. Help in the form of A. P. Hill's Division had to be sent Jackson as a precaution; more reinforcements must be put on trains as soon as word of Burnside's sailing was received.

There soon was a third and even more exciting possibility: Northern newspapers began to hint that McClellan was about to leave his camp on James River and unite his army with Pope's in an overwhelming attack on the Confederates. If that happened, there would indeed be a race—between Lee by land to Jackson and McClellan by water to Pope.

At first there was a period of uncertainty. Jackson thought he saw a prospect of striking part of Pope's Army before the other Federal divisions could arrive. On the 9th of August, a frightfully hot day, Jackson attacked and won a victory that took its name from nearby Cedar Mountain. Two days later Jackson had to withdraw to the Rapidan River in the face of larger numbers than he could hope to defeat. Soon Lee became satisfied that Burnside was to join Pope. Almost simultaneously Lee decided there was truth to the reports that McClellan was preparing to move also. Lee accordingly took Longstreet's men and started by train to reinforce Jackson. The remaining troops were to move as soon as it was certain that McClellan was leaving James River.

The race was on. Everything depended now on two things. One was the speed with which the Confederates moved in comparison with the Federals. The other was the success Lee had in getting teamwork from his men when next they met Pope and King and Burnside and such of McClellan's soldiers as might reach Pope ahead of Lee. If the Confederates did not put into the fight everything they had, they were certain to be beaten by the larger Federal Army.

The events of the next fortnight were among the proudest achievements of Confederate history. First of all, at a place called Verdiersville, "Jeb" Stuart barely escaped capture while he was awaiting the arrival of his troops. Then, overnight, Pope withdrew to the Rappahannock River because some of his men surprised Lee's signal station and captured dispatches which showed that Lee was trying to catch the Federals between the Rapidan and the Rappahannock. Next, on the night of August 23, "Jeb" Stuart raided the field headquarters of Pope at Catlett's Station and took the General's dress uniform in exchange for the hat he had lost at Verdiersville. In Pope's tent, also, Stuart found many military papers. Some of these confirmed reports that McClellan was expecting to join Pope, who was seeking to hold the Rappahannock River till the arrival of the Union troops from James River.

Lee now made another interesting decision: He concluded that he could delay the arrival of McClellan and give himself time to bring up the last of his troops from Richmond if he forced Pope to retreat northward and thereby to lengthen the distance McClellan had to march. How could Pope be compelled to retreat? Lee thought the surest means would be to send Confederate troops to the rear of Pope, where they could tear up the railroad and prevent the shipment of supplies to the Army of Virginia. When the Federals became hungry, they would have to withdraw.

On the afternoon of the 24th of August, Lee decided to make the attempt. "Stonewall" Jackson was to take about 23,000 men and was to march northward by roads beyond the reach of the Federals. Then, at some suitable place, Jackson was to turn eastward and strike for the Orange and Alexandria railroad from which Pope got all his supplies. Jackson slipped quietly away on August 25 and began one of the most celebrated marches in American history. Lee waited until the next day and then he followed Jackson. He did this because he knew "Stonewall" would need help if Pope found out what was happening and tried to destroy Jackson's Army.

Late that afternoon, August 26, on the road, Lee received great news: Jackson had marched fifty-four miles in two days without encountering any Federals. He had passed through Bull Run Mountain, at a pass called Thoroughfare Gap, and had gone on to the railway. At Bristoe Station his men had met and had scattered a Union guard and then had wrecked several railroad trains that had been passing at a time when the crews had no idea any rebels were near. From Bristoe during the night of August 26–27, some of Jackson's troops had moved up the track to Manassas Junction. There they found tons and tons of every sort of food a hungry Confederate could crave. All this meant, in military terms, that Pope's lines of supply were cut and that he would have to retreat. The Confederates with Lee must hurry on. Otherwise, hastening northward, Pope might throw all his troops on Jackson's 23,000.

Over a dusty road, General James Longstreet moved all the remaining Confederates that had arrived from Richmond. In mid-afternoon of the 28th, Longstreet's men reached Thoroughfare Gap. They had no such good fortune as Jackson had enjoyed in finding the pass empty. This time Federal infantry held the gap and gave every indication of resisting attack.

For a time things looked black. If Lee were held up a day, in front of that pass, Jackson might have to fight for his life. Fortunately, the Federals on the mountain soon changed their minds and withdrew. Two Confederate divisions slept on the east side of Thoroughfare that night. The next morning, August 29, as Lee pushed forward, he and his companions could see smoke rising where they thought Jackson's Army must be, but they could not hear his cannon. Before long, the officers at the front of the Confederate column saw some horsemen on the edge of a wood ahead of them. Everyone wanted to know whether this cavalry were Confederate or Union—whether they would get news of Jackson or have a fight. Doubt remained for a moment only. Then, as the mounted troops rode out, the breeze opened their flag. It was the Confederate Stars and Bars and it was carried by some of "Jeb" Stuart's men.

Stuart reported that Jackson had fought a hard battle the previous evening near a place called Groveton and now was holding off the enemy in front of Sudley's Ford. Lee hurried on to reenforce Jackson and soon had his men forming a line that looked to the East and at a wide angle to Jackson's front, which faced South. Some of Jackson's men had observed the approach of troops, whom they had not been able to identify. A courier rode out, halted, took a quick view, and then galloped back to Jackson's line. "It's Longstreet," he cried.

It was well that Longstreet had arrived, because the Federals were preparing a furious attack on Jackson. He beat it off that evening of August 29, but the splendid South Carolina troops on the extreme left of his line had to stand many attacks. The commander, General Maxey Gregg, took out his grandfather's scimitar, used in the Revolutionary War, and strode among his soldiers. "Let us die here, my men," he kept saying, "let us die here." Many of them fell with their hot guns in their grimy hands, but the survivors, with help from other units, threw back the last assault.

Lee had felt that Longstreet should assist Jackson during this fight. Longstreet waited because he was not certain about conditions near his own lines. Soon the two Generals were told by "Jeb" Stuart that Federal troops were arriving in front of Longstreet and that they almost certainly belonged to Porter's corps. At the name, the soldiers must have straightened their shoulders: Porter's corps belonged to Mc-

Clellan's Army, some parts of which already were known to have reached Pope. If Porter represented the main force of McClellan and was just then coming on the field, the Confederates had won the race, but how narrowly! It had been a matter of two or three hours at most.

A strange silence prevailed on the Confederate front during the early morning of August 30. Then, about 8 o'clock, the Federals opened a slow artillery fire. Later in the day they quickened this cannonade and then, in the afternoon, they resumed their attacks on Jackson. This time Longstreet had no reason to wait. He opened with many guns near the angle where his line joined Jackson's and then he hurled his gray infantry against the Federals. Every regiment seemed to start forward at the same instant. Instead of a division attacking here and another attacking yonder an hour later, there was what Lee sought, what the situation required—complete teamwork. In the face of it, though some Federal troops stood gallantly, most of them broke and ran. Pursuit continued till darkness stopped it.

Rain on the 31st held the Confederates in the mud. They undertook on September 1 to reopen the struggle, but the Union troops, beating off attacks, retired toward the Washington defences. Lee felt it was futile to follow. The forts around the Federal capital were strong; the Southerners had come so far that they could not bring up food and ammunition easily from Richmond. Nor could they live on the surrounding country. It had been picked bare.

Instead, then, of wasting the time and the lives of his men in front of Washington, Lee decided to enter Maryland. In that State, where many persons sympathized with the Confederate cause, the army might get some recruits. It certainly could hope to find food there and to spare Virginia and the South.

This Maryland Expedition was a dangerous thing to undertake. Lee's men were tired. Some of them had been marching and fighting since the last week in June. Thousands had worn out their shoes and had bruised their feet. Others felt that it was wrong to invade the North. They had taken up arms to drive out the invaders of their own soil and they did not want to do the thing for which they condemned their enemy.

The extent of this feeling and the bad condition of the men's feet were not known when the army crossed the Potomac on the 5th and 6th of September and headed for Frederick. At the beginning of this "invasion of the North" everything was gay. The bands played "Maryland, my Maryland" over and over again; the men raised their famous "rebel yell," which was the high, sustained cry of foxhunters; Marylanders whose hearts were with the South brought out provisions and cool water and had smiles and cheers for the ragged Confederates.

By the 9th of September the situation lost its pleasant color. Lee had hoped that when he entered Maryland the Federal garrison at Harpers Ferry, Virginia, would abandon the place. In this he was disappointed. The Federals remained in the picturesque town at the junction of the Potomac and the Shenandoah Rivers. So long as they stayed there, they were in position to move out and attack wagons that might be moving down the Shenandoah Valley to carry supplies to the Confederate Army.

Lee decided that he had to get the Federals out of Harpers Ferry. To do this surely and swiftly he must use a large part of his Army. It would be risky to leave the remainder of the army where it was, close to the town of Frederick. Besides, food was getting scarce there. The troops that were not sent to Harpers Ferry must be moved somewhere that provisions could be found or brought readily from Virginia. For a number of military reasons, it seemed best to move the troops twenty-seven miles northwestward to Hagerstown.

All this was started in the manner Lee wished. Six divisions of the army were sent on the 10th to attack Harpers Ferry from three sides and to compel its defenders to surrender. Jackson at the outset commanded three of these Confederate divisions. When they got in touch with one another around Harpers Ferry he would head all of them. Lee started for Hagerstown with the remaining four divisions.

Before Harpers Ferry could be captured, Lee heard from "Jeb" Stuart that the Federal Army was moving westward from Washington toward Frederick. This surprised all the Confederate leaders, because they knew that the Union troops were again under General McClellan who always prepared everything with great care and moved slowly.

On hearing that McClellan was coming toward him, Lee had to hurry back one of his divisions under D. H. Hill to South Mountain. This was the strongest nearby position a few men could hold against many and it was, also, the place where a stand had to be made to protect one of the three columns that had marched off to Harpers Ferry. This column, which was under General Lafayette McLaws, had gone to a place called Maryland Heights, a great bluff across the Potomac River from the town. Any Union army moving unhindered over South Mountain could come up behind McLaws and capture all his troops.

On the 14th of September, General Hill tried to keep the Federals from crossing at South Mountain. He put up a good fight but he had too many men against him. Even when Lee hurried back from Hagerstown with Longstreet's troops, there did not seem to be much chance of keeping the Federals East of the mountain. While Lee and his Generals were discussing their prospect, they received bad news. Farther down the mountain, at Crampton's Gap, the Unionists already had crossed and were in rear of McLaws.

This looked as if the divided Confederates were to be beaten and perhaps destroyed. Orders were given for the quickest possible return to Virginia, but before these orders could be executed, Lee received from Jackson a report which indicated that Harpers Ferry would be captured the next morning. If that happened, then McLaws, when attacked from the rear, could get across the Potomac to the captured town or could go up the river and join Lee again. Jackson could reunite also. The danger to Lee seemed to be past. He might march into Western Maryland, collect all his troops there, and beat McClellan's Army when it was a long way from Washington.

The soldiers who remained with the army were equal to this call. On the 15th of September Lee marched them across Antietam Creek and placed them on the ridges that run back from the creek to the quiet little town of Sharpsburg. Everything appeared to be favorable until, later in the day, the cavalry sent word that McClellan was advancing rapidly and in great strength as if he were determined to fight it out at once. Lee continued to wonder what had happened to make the slow-moving, cautious McClellan so anxious to join battle. Not until weeks afterward did Lee learn the reason. It was this: In Frederick, a Union soldier had picked up a package of three cigars, which had fallen from some Confederate officer's pocket. These cigars were wrapped in a paper on which there was a good deal of writing. Naturally the soldier looked to see what it was and saw to his amazement that he had in his hands a copy of Lee's order for the movement of the army to Harpers Ferry and to Hagerstown. General McClellan received the paper and instantly knew as much about Lee's plans as if he had been in Lee's tent when the plan had been discussed. The Union commander was hurrying now to reach Lee before Jackson and the other troops returned from Harpers Ferry.

It was going to be another close race. Jackson sent word that he had taken Harpers Ferry on the morning of the 15th and had captured the whole garrison, which proved to number about 11,000 men. Obedient to orders, Jackson would start as soon as possible to rejoin Lee. By the hardest marching, three of Jackson's divisions arrived on the afternoon of the 16th about the time the Federals began to move across the creek and to spread themselves out for action. One division of Jackson, under A. P. Hill, had remained at Harpers Ferry to parole the prisoners. McLaws had come across the Potomac to Harpers Ferry and was starting for Sharpsburg with his two divisions. If he and Hill arrived in time for the battle, there was a prospect the Federals could be beaten off. If McLaws and Hill were delayed, then there was no sense in denying what every soldier could see for himself. The hardest fighting and the most perfect teamwork would be demanded if the army was to escape defeat. Rout would be ruin. The Potomac River was only three miles behind the lines the Confederates occupied.

At dawn on the 17th of September, the Federals opened the Battle of Sharpsburg or The Antietam. It proved to be the bloodiest one-day fight that ever occurred on this continent. The struggle began on the left, swept Jackson back with heavy losses and then grew furious on the centre. Precisely when it was at its worst there, McLaws's men arrived and helped to prevent disaster, but even with this help the centre would have been wrecked had not the Southerners fought more desperately than perhaps they ever had before. The contest then shifted to the Confederate right, which was held by a few thousand men only. They were being overwhelmed when through the dust of the road and under a red, low-slanting sun, A. P. Hill arrived with the very last men Lee could hope to put into the fight. These troops hurled back the Federals and put an end to the battle.

On the ghastly field that night, all the Confederates wondered whether McClellan would attack the next day. If he did, could the weakened Confederates withstand him? Lee did not believe McClellan would renew the fight, but he resolved to stand his ground and to defend his line to the last hour should the Union troops challenge him again. The result bore out Lee's judgment of his opponent. McClellan failed to renew the fight on the 18th. Lee waited till night and then got back across the Potomac with all his guns and all except his worst wounded men. The Maryland Expedition was over. It had been a narrow escape from disaster but it and Second Manassas had proved one thing: Under Lee, the army now had developed teamwork. The army fought as a unit, not as separate divisions.

CHAPTER ELEVEN

Far-Southerners Have a Strange Reward

WHEN LEE returned to Southern soil after the Maryland Expedition, he had been in command of the Army of Northern Virginia for about three and a half months. During that time he had made the army into a new fighting machine which had absolute confidence in itself and in him. Critics and Northern enemies might say that some of the seven battles of the army had been in reality defeats—as at Mechanicsville—and that Sharpsburg at best was a tie. The men who fought under Lee would not admit it: They always won under General Lee, they said, and they always would. This belief created morale that made every single unit of the army stronger than a like number of men would have been without like confidence in their ability to win. The soldiers knew, also, that General Lee would provide for them everything that the small resources of the Confederacy could furnish. "He looks after his men," the soldiers said and in that simple sentence gave their idea of what a real leader should be. Lee might be compelled to order long marches and costly assaults but he always had the ability to make the best of everything, to soften hardship and to keep wounds and losses low. That was the feeling of the men. In a single summer they had built up tremendous, unshakable faith in Lee whom, in June, they had denounced as the "King of Spades."

Lee had learned during that same summer of combat to know his men and most of the officers who had charge of his troops. The commanding General had as much confidence in them as they had in him. Their patience, their good humor, their willingness to meet his every demand on them, and their quickness in learning the art of war had won his full respect. He avoided comparisons, of course, but later he said that he believed the men knew their duties better than their officers knew how to lead them.

This did not mean that he failed to appreciate the fine leaders among his Generals, his Colonels and his Majors. As Lee became better acquainted with these officers, he saw that he had a few men of first-rate ability among them. Others, he discovered, had received professional training as soldiers and knew what to do in emergencies. These men, or at least some of them, would develop into good leaders. Still others would learn enough to direct a regiment, but they might not have either the knowledge of military matters or the type of mind required to handle large bodies of men with least loss and greatest success. Gradually, too, Lee came to realize that he had among the younger officers some whom the soldiers called natural born fighting men. In a terrible battle the next year a wounded Georgian defined what he and his comrades meant by that term. Asked the name of his command, he replied: "I belong to Gordon's old Brigade, Cap'n. Did you ever see the Gin'ral in battle? He's most the prettiest thing you ever did see on a field of fight. It'ud put fight into a whipped chicken just to look at him!" The sad thing was that many of the bravest men took unnecessary risks under fire. In all the battles, and especially at Sharpsburg, many had been shot down who could not be replaced easily if at all.

At this period of the war, the autumn of 1862, there were five men in the army whom Lee considered his ablest and most useful leaders.

James Longstreet stood first. He was the senior division commander and apparently the best all-around soldier. Longstreet was not a fast marcher but he kept his head in the wildest struggle and he seemed always to know where his troops were, what they were doing and what they could be expected to accomplish. In addition to these fine qualities, Longstreet kept his staff and his subordinates in good spirits. He seldom had any bitter quarrels in his command at this stage of his experience. All the army business that came under his eye was well and promptly handled. "Old Pete," or "Peter" Longstreet, as the men styled him, was a thoroughly reliable soldier. Lee sometimes called him "my war-horse."

On equal footing with Longstreet in many respects, and superior to him in some was "Stonewall" Jackson. When Jackson had failed to accomplish in front of Richmond everything that had been expected of him, some had said that he was ambitious and was determined to have an army of his own. Lee did not find this true. He saw Jackson as a man wholly devoted to the Southern cause, an intense patriot and a conscientious Christian who never spared himself or his men. Over and over again in August, and many times afterward Jackson repaid Lee for this confidence. "Stonewall" was quick to understand what his commander wanted and prompt in executing orders. He marched fast; he fought furiously. Longstreet liked to maneuver until he could make the enemy attack him in a strong position. Jackson always went after the enemy. At heart he was an offensive fighter. His defects while not numerous, were serious. He was not a particularly good judge of men and sometimes selected staff officers or brigade commanders who did not meet the requirements of combat. More serious than this was Jackson's exaggerated conception of duty. In the belief that no man ever could do everything that the Lord required of him, Jackson strove to do his utmost and to hold all others to the same unyielding standards. He was apt to punish severely all shortcomings and even to pursue a man. Sometimes Jackson acted as if he felt he failed in his duty if he forgave a man for failing. This characteristic created resentment among some of Jackson's officers, but his grim person, his zeal for battle and his little oddities of behavior made his men talk about him endlessly and always with enthusiasm. Some of them continued to believe him a half crazy genius. Others regarded him as a blend of Joshua and of Oliver Cromwell.

Two other men whom Lee put highest at this time were A. P. Hill and a fine, friendly, unselfish South Carolinian named Richard Heron Anderson. In the judgment of Lee, Hill and Anderson were developing steadily. They gave every indication that when the test came, they could lead more men than they had in their respective divisions. "Jeb" Stuart was the other leader who stood first in Lee's estimation. He thought Stuart almost an ideal soldier in cheerfulness, industry and physical endurance.

Justice was one of the strongest expressions of Lee's character, when judging these five or any other officers. Lee never failed to consider fairly everything that could be said in their behalf. In October, 1862, he had to decide which of his lieutenants best could be trusted with higher rank and larger responsibility. One reason for this was that he had to replace the numerous officers killed or disabled at Sharpsburg. The other reason was that the Confederate Congress had provided the new rank of Lieutenant General between the existing rank of Major General and the full grade of General. This was done because experience was showing the need of officers who could supervise several divisions, though they might not be qualified or needed as army commanders. The divisions linked together in this manner were to be corps; commanders of corps were to be Lieutenant Generals. Lee was notified that he could recommend two such officers for service in his army. Without hesitation he endorsed Longstreet and Jackson and said that if more were needed in his army, Hill and Anderson would be qualified. "Jeb" Stuart already had been made Major General, which Lee considered as high a rank as an officer in command of a limited force of cavalry should have.

In recommending other officers to appointment as brigade or division commanders, Lee did not say why he declined to urge the promotion of some men. He took many things into account, but there were two failings he always considered a bar to the high promotion of an officer. One was lack of self-control, especially in the use of intoxicants. "I am sorry," he said once, when asked to advance a certain officer, "but I cannot trust a man to command others who cannot command himself." The second failing was what he called "croaking." By that he meant to describe the state of mind that always sees disaster ahead and magnifies the difficulties that have to be encountered. Lee believed that good cheer was an essential to successful command. He seldom gave higher rank to "croakers" and sometimes he quietly got rid of those he found among his higher officers.

When the necessary promotions were made in October and November, 1862, Lee divided his army into two corps. The First was placed under Longstreet; the Second was Jackson's. All the cavalry remained under Stuart. Within a few weeks after this new organization was established, it was subjected to the test of battle. President Lincoln became dissatisfied over McClellan's failure to pursue Lee after the Battle of Sharpsburg, and on the 7th of November, he ordered the General to turn over command of the Army of the Potomac to Maj. Gen. Ambrose E. Burnside. As a result of the change of commanders, the scene of action was changed, also. General Burnside moved eastward and placed his army on the northern bank of the Rappahannock River, opposite Fredericksburg. Lee followed him there. Before day-

light, December 11, General Burnside tried to put down bridges made
of boats—pontoon bridges—so that he could get his troops across to
the side of the river the Confederates were holding. That bank of
the Rappahannock was held by Mississippi and Florida boys, all of
whom were good marksmen. For a long time they kept the Federals
from finishing the pontoon bridges but at last the Confederates had to
fall back. One of the bitterest of the smaller fights that occurred while
the Confederates were leaving the town was waged by some Mississippi soldiers under a former student of the Harvard Law School. He
had learned in some manner that the troops pursuing him were Massachusetts boys led by his former classmate and chum. He simply *had*
to beat his friend.

On the 13th of December, General Burnside undertook to drive
the Confederates from the high ground behind Fredericksburg. The
struggle that day was called the Battle of Fredericksburg, but it was
not really a battle. It was a massacre. Burnside simply threw away the
lives of thousands of his men in the face of the rifle and cannon fire
of a strong and confident Southern army in an ideal position. From
an eminence that ever since has been called "Lee's Hill," the Confederate commander watched the men in blue rush bravely forward
and then, leaving hundreds of dead, fall back again. Lee's eyes flashed.
His battle blood rose in his veins. Turning to Longstreet, he said
earnestly, "It is well that war is so terrible—we should grow too fond
of it!"

It *was* terrible. Especially after the battle, when the excitement was
past, any right-minded man would have wept to walk across the field
and to see the dead and the dying. One 19-year-old boy, a Sergeant
of the Second South Carolina, Richard Kirkland, became so distressed
at the pathetic cries for "Water, water" that he got permission from
his General, climbed out of the trench, and for an hour and a half car-

ried water to the fallen. During all that time, though he was in range of the Northerners, not one shot was fired at him. Kirkland did not stop until he had given water to every man within reach.

Some of the wounded were taken later into their lines, but on the night of December 15–16, while a strong wind was carrying the sound away from the Confederates, the Union Army got back across the Potomac. General Lee was grieved, because, as he wrote, the battle "did not go far enough to satisfy me." The men felt the same way, but those who had come from the Far South had two special rewards besides that of a military success. One reward was a first sight of snow. The other was a glorious Aurora Borealis on the night after the main battle. "We enthusiastic young fellows," one Confederate said afterward, "felt that the heavens were hanging out banners and streamers and setting off fireworks in honor of our victory."

CHAPTER TWELVE

A Great Victory at a Terrible Price

AFTER HIS DEFEAT at Fredericksburg, General Burnside made one more attempt to attack the Confederates, but the roads were so heavy and the hillsides so slippery that he scarcely got to the bank of the Rappahannock. After this "Mud March," as it was called, the infantry fighting ended for the season of cold weather, though the cavalry made several raids.

As the army thus went into winter quarters, General Lee had his tent and those of his staff set up in thick pine woods not far from Hamilton's Crossing on the railroad below Fredericksburg. He lived simply and on plain food, about which he sometimes joked with his young officers. When one of them said that the biscuits were indigestible, Lee said, "They will stick by you longer." On another occasion, there was so small a piece of bacon with the cabbage served for dinner that all those present, including guests, politely declined to have any of it. The next day, when no visitors were at the table, Lee remembered the meat and asked for it. His cook had to confess, "That was borrowed bacon and I have sent it back to the man I got it from."

General Jackson lived somewhat more comfortably. Because one of his ears gave him trouble when he camped out of doors in winter, his doctor ordered him to sleep indoors. A generous family offered him the use of Moss Neck, a fine mansion on the Rappahannock, but he would accept no more than the use of a small building in the yard.

This had been the office of the owner of the plantation, who had a great fondness for race horses and chicken fights. On the walls of the office were numerous sporting prints about which "Jeb" Stuart often teased Jackson. Those pictures, said Stuart, reflected Jackson's real tastes. That was why he chose the office. Everybody laughed at this in the knowledge that Jackson was a Presbyterian deacon and a man of the strictest views of "worldly amusements."

In spite of Jackson's better quarters, the winter was a hard one for him as well as for Lee. Before Jackson had come to Fredericksburg, he had heard that a baby girl had been born to him, but he had never been at home during the war and, of course, he had never seen her. He kept hoping that Mrs. Jackson could visit him in the spring and bring the baby with her.

In yearning for his own child, he had great pleasure in the company of a little girl, Janie Corbin, who lived in the "big house," at Moss Neck. On her visits to Jackson, he would sit with her on the floor in front of the fire in the office, and would cut out paper dolls for her. Sometimes he would cut a thick pile of them with their hands joined, and he would tell her these were men of the "'Stonewall Brigade," his favorite troops.

Janie had lovely, golden hair which often fell over her eyes and bothered her. She would shake it back impatiently. Jackson noticed this one day, got up from the floor, took his military hat, clipped from it the shining gold-braid band, and put this around Janie's curls. She wore that braid, as if it had been a coronet, every time she came to see the General, but that was not long. He left in March and heard to his dismay that Janie was too sick to say good-bye. The next day she died of scarlet fever. The gold braid was saved. It is now in the Confederate Museum of Richmond.

The life of the men in the ranks was very different from that of

Jackson during the winter of 1862–63. Nearly all the soldiers lived in little wooden huts they built with timber cut from the hills. A few of the men preferred tents, to which they built chimneys. Some of the soldiers on high ground found dug-outs more comfortable. The men constructed chapels as well as barracks and held every imaginable form of meeting. Living in the face of death, many of the soldiers found help and comfort in religion. Prayer meetings were held daily; revival services were always in progress among some of the troops. They had theatres, too. On week days there were concerts, dramatic performances, debates, minstrel shows and mock trials. When the ground was snow-covered, there were great snow-ball battles in which the men charged and counter-charged and made flank attacks as if they really were fighting. For this exercise there was little enough food and that chiefly a monotonous diet of bread and meat. Many of the men living in nearby States had occasional boxes from home, which they shared with their friends. Soldiers from far-off States—Mississippi, Louisiana, Arkansas and Texas—naturally received fewer boxes and consequently suffered most because of the smallness of the ration.

During the long gray winter, a strange change occurred in the landscape. To provide huts and fuel, trees were cut from hundreds of acres. Natives who never had seen from their windows the homes of any of their neighbors discovered that new vistas had been opened and that other residences were visible. It looked as if the very face of nature was being marred. Another change that winter was in the horses and mules, on which the army was in large measure dependent. All the teams that possibly could be spared from the army were sent into districts where forage could be had, but many had to be kept near the front. These animals were thin and always hungry—so hungry that often they gnawed the bark off the trees. It was an unpleasant sight around the camps—every tree stripped of bark as high as horses could use their teeth.

General Lee had a great love of horses and he shared the soldiers' grief at the suffering of the animals. Many other griefs were his, because he bore much of the burden of the army on his own shoulders. He had to arrange that winter for the emancipation of Mr. Custis's slaves, as provided by the will of his father-in-law, and he found this a difficult matter because the servants were widely scattered. The shortage of rations was an agony to Lee. "His theory, expressed on many occasions," wrote one of his officers, "was that the private soldiers—men who fought without the stimulus of rank, emolument, or individual renown—were the most meritorious class of the army, and that they deserved and should receive the utmost respect and consideration." When they had, instead, hunger and cold, Lee was miserable. All his individual suffering and losses were as nothing, in his mind, compared with theirs.

Another Army besides his own was on his heart. Confederates under General John C. Pemberton were defending the important heights of Vicksburg, on the Mississippi River. If Vicksburg were lost, the Confederate States would be cut in half. Lee perceived this more clearly than most men did, and he spent many an anxious night of prayer. The accumulation of strains at last proved too heavy for him. He developed throat trouble and then some heart affection which his physicians had difficulty in diagnosing. From March 30 until after the end of the first week in April he was confined to a room in a private home. For another week he was half-incapacitated.

When Lee was well enough to resume his full duties, spring had come to the Valley of the Rappahannock. New hope was rising, the confident soldiers were getting restless—and the enemy was stirring.

General Burnside had been relieved of command of the Federal Army of the Potomac. It was now in charge of Maj. Gen. Joseph Hooker, "Fighting Joe" Hooker as he was called. Those who knew him said he was not a man to sit indefinitely on the hills of Stafford County, opposite Fredericksburg. Hooker would attack. That was certain. The only questions were, where would the Federal commander strike and when?

To get the quickest possible answer to that question, General Lee had his cavalry spread for a long distance up and down the Rappahannock, and opposite some of the places where the river was shallow enough for the Federals to "ford" or wade across, he had infantry. He was sure his men would do their utmost. They always had been too few to meet the enemy on equal terms. Now the Confederate Army was weaker by two divisions, which had been sent South of James River under General Longstreet to deal with a strong Federal force there. When Hooker attacked, Lee might have only Jackson's Corps, two of Longstreet's Divisions, Stuart's Cavalry and the greater part of the artillery. If the Confederates were not outnumbered more than three to two in this campaign, they would be lucky. The odds might be two to one.

General Hooker was as bold as Lee had thought he might be. On the 29th of April, 1863, Federal troops crossed on pontoons below Fredericksburg, precisely as they had in December. A very large Union force was known to be on the northern bank of the Rappahannock, northwest of the town. When these infantry divisions moved to the southern side of the stream, as they most certainly would, they first would pass a dreary district called "the P'ison Fields" and then they would enter a great forest of mixed hardwood and pine, known as the Wilderness of Spotsylvania or, for short, the Wilderness. In that semijungle, there were many places where the underbrush was so thick a person could not see 100 yards in any direction. An entire army might be hidden in that sombre, silent woodland.

Lee had to deal, then, with two forces—with Hooker in the Wilderness, and with Federals who had crossed the river below Fredericksburg. These troops were found to be under General John Sedgwick, a gentleman and a good soldier. If Lee marched all his troops to meet Hooker, of course Sedgwick would follow and would pounce on Lee's back. Lee considered all this and then made a simple decision: He would leave some infantry and a strong force of artillery under the command of Jubal A. Early on the heights behind Fredericksburg, and he would rely on the strength of the hills and the vigilance of the troops to keep Sedgwick from advancing to meet Hooker. While this was being done at Fredericksburg, Lee intended to take all his other troops and go straight after "Fighting Joe."

To head the troops who were to meet Hooker, the choice of Lee was "Stonewall" Jackson. That officer was having at the time the pleasant visit to which he long had looked forward. Mrs. Jackson and the baby had come to see him. He spent with them all the time he could spare from the army, and he never seemed to tire of sitting and looking at his little girl. Now that he had to hurry away to fight, he regretfully said good-bye to them and left one of his officers to see that they went that day by train to Richmond, where they would be out of danger.

At the head of his troops on the morning of May 1, Jackson started for the Wilderness. He had not reached the eastern edge of the forest when he came on Gen. "Dick" Anderson's men who had gone ahead. Already these troops of Anderson's were beginning a fight with the Federals. Jackson brought his own men forward and started an attack. Soon Lee joined him, but left the handling of the troops to him.

General Hooker had moved fast. His officers had supported him well. He had a great part of his Army out of the Wilderness and on open ground where his greater numbers would count most. Jackson was going to have a fierce and bloody struggle. While all the officers were saying this, a strange thing happened: The Federals began slowly to withdraw toward the Wilderness. After having gained a great advantage by getting clear of that tangle, Hooker was retreating into it. The Confederates did not know what to think of this. Some of Hooker's own generals were equally surprised. The only explanation they could give, then or thereafter, was that Hooker had lost his nerve.

Lee and Jackson and their troops followed the Federals into the Wilderness until they were halted by Union fire from the woods. Several engineers then crept forward to see how strong the position of the enemy was. Before nightfall these officers returned and shook their heads grimly. The Unionists were building earthworks and log fortifications in the thickets. Artillery could not be employed against them. It would be almost impossible to drive the enemy back through the woods to the river.

About the time of these reports, Gen. Fitz Lee of the cavalry rode up and gave more encouraging news. He and his men had been a long way to the West through the Wilderness and had reached the end of the Union line. It did not rest on the river or on any hill or ridge. As soldiers would say, "the flank was in the air." If the Confederate infantry could move secretly to the West through the woods and could get to the place Fitz Lee had reached, they might be able to destroy a large part of Hooker's Army.

Were there roads by which such a march could be conducted? That question Lee discussed with Jackson while the two sat by a little fire in the deep pine woods. After a while the two Generals concluded that roads probably did exist in that part of the Wilderness. Lee asked Jackson to find out all that could be learned about trails and tracks and roads. Then Lee lay down under a lofty pine tree, covered himself with his overcoat and went to sleep.

When Lee woke up early the next morning, May 2, Jackson was sitting on a cracker box by a little fire and was studying eagerly the reports of young officers who had found a route by which they thought the troops could move to the West without being seen.

"General Jackson," said Lee, after greeting his lieutenant, "what do you propose to do?"

"Go around here," Jackson answered, and with his finger traced the course of roads and trails through the woods.

"What do you propose to make this movement with?" Lee continued.

"With my whole corps."

"What will you leave me?"

"The Divisions of Anderson and McLaws."

That was a startling proposal sure enough! Jackson wanted to take 28,000 men, march off, and leave Lee not more than half that number with which to fight perhaps 50,000 Federals. Still, if Jackson were going to attack at all, he must have sufficient troops to beat the enemy thoroughly. If that involved long chances and hard fighting for the Confederates who remained behind, Lee would take the risk and do the fighting. Without saying a word to indicate that his task would be a heavy one, Lee answered simply, "Well, go on." Jackson explained the details.

Soon everything was arranged. About 7 o'clock, the first of Jackson's gray regiments began to move past the edge of the woods where Lee was waiting. In a short time Jackson himself rode up, saluted and drew rein for a moment. The two exchanged a few words. Jackson, his eyes already aflame, pointed down the road on which his men were marching. Lee nodded. "Stonewall" touched his horse. A few minutes later, his gaunt form had disappeared among the trees. If either he or Lee thought this interview different in any way from a hundred other meetings, neither man gave any indication of it. They parted, as so often they had, in the expectation that they would see each other again, that night or the next morning, on the field of battle.

The day did not prove as hard as Lee had expected. In the thickets, the Federals seemed quite content to rest and to await Confederate attack. Not a word came from Jackson until midday. Then a courier reported that Jackson's wagon train had been attacked. As no further report arrived, Lee took for granted that Jackson would beat off the attack, but he sent some troops toward the point where the trains were exposed.

Next news from Jackson was a note to the effect that the enemy had made a stand at a place about two miles from a clearing in the Wilderness known as Chancellorsville. Jackson said he was preparing to attack. "I trust," he added, "that an ever kind Providence will bless us with great success." Lee read and calculated the time and distance of the march. If everything went well, the sound of Jackson's guns soon would be heard from the West.

While Lee watched his own line, and waited and strained his ears, another report was brought—but from the opposite direction, and a bad report at that. The troops left at Fredericksburg to watch Sedgwick had given up their position and had started a march to join Lee. An officer who had been sent to Fredericksburg that morning by Lee had misunderstood his orders and had told General Early to leave the hills and to move to Lee's assistance. What Lee had intended to order was that Early come to his assistance if the Federals at Fredericksburg disappeared. The mistake might have terrible consequences. A messenger must hurry back to Early at once and tell him to return to Fredericksburg and hold the heights. Otherwise Sedgwick might be marching against Lee's rear before Jackson could hit Hooker.

Jackson at that very time was preparing to strike. All day he had urged his willing troops to keep their fast pace on the narrow trails of the green Wilderness. "Press on, men," he kept saying. "Close up, men, close up!" Now, he had reached a low, wooded ridge beyond the Federal right flank. He was facing East and had in front of him a road that pointed like an arrow in the direction of his advance. From what he had been able to see, few of the unsuspecting Federals were looking to the West. Most of them were facing South, as if they awaited an attack from that direction.

The Confederates had been forming three lines, one behind another, on either side of the road. Jackson was not certain whether the men were in position. He took out his watch and observed the time. It was 5:15. "Are you ready, General Rodes?" he asked of the young officer who was going to lead the attack.

"Yes, sir," Rodes replied.

"You can go forward then," Jackson said quietly.

Rodes nodded to another officer, who gave a signal. Instantly through the forest the notes of a bugle rang out. At the sound, the men began to crash their way toward the enemy. Federals at that time were smoking and chatting around their fires while their cooks prepared supper. Most of these Union soldiers were Germans who had been hired to fight. Some of them had been so short a time in the United States that they could not speak or understand English. The first they knew of the approach of Jackson was a sudden scamper through the camps of deer and rabbits which were running to escape the long line of men in the woods. Before that sudden and furious attack, the Federals at once gave way in flight almost as mad as that of the wild animals. In a few minutes Jackson was rolling up the entire Federal right and was pushing it in the direction of Lee's two divisions. In the whole of the war there had been no more successful an attack, no greater surprise for the enemy.

As soon as Lee heard from the West the echo of Jackson's guns, he had all the troops with him make a demonstration as if they, too, were strong and were about to attack. It was nothing more than a noisy bluff but it served its purpose. When night fell, the Union troops opposite Lee still were hugging their position. None of them, so far as the Confederates could see, had been shifted to the right to oppose Jackson's attack. Lee continued to threaten an advance, hurled shell here, sent rattling infantry volleys yonder, and all the while kept his eyes on the western skies which flashed and flamed with the reflection of the fire from Jackson's cannon. It was midnight before the light and the sound died away. Then, as a mysterious silence fell over the Wilderness, the whip-poor-wills began their weird song. It was enough to make a man shudder with loneliness, though he lay among ten thousand on the ground.

About 2:30, while the dirge of the whip-poor-wills still was in the air, Lee was aroused by another sound. One of his staff officers was talking with an officer who had just arrived.

"Who is there?" Lee inquired.

"It is Captain Wilbourn," the staff officer said.

Wilbourn was Jackson's signal officer and, as he sat down by Lee, he had a brave but dreadful story to tell. Jackson had driven the Federals before him with great slaughter until it had been too dark to fight any more. Then, when he had gone forward to see where the enemy was, he had been wounded three times in the arm and hand. A volley from Confederates who failed to heed an order to cease fire was responsible.

Lee groaned aloud. "Ah, Captain," he said, "any victory is dearly bought which deprives us of the services of General Jackson, even for a short time!" When Wilbourn went on to describe how Jackson had been carried to the rear and had been placed in the hands of surgeons, Lee was so much disturbed that he had to stop the Captain. "Don't talk about it," he begged. "Thank God it is no worse!"

With the dawn of May 3, the battle was renewed. In place of the wounded and half conscious Jackson, the vigorous "Jeb" Stuart commanded the troops who had delivered the surprise attack from the West. Lee had now to press from the South and had to extend his line until he could join Stuart's men. It was done perfectly under the immediate direction of "Dick" Anderson. About noon, as the two Confederate forces united and closed on the centre of Hooker's position, General Lee rode into the clearing around the Chancellor House, which was burning like a torch at a celebration. One of Lee's staff best described a scene which men said afterward was the high noon of the Southern Confederacy: "The fierce soldiers with their faces blackened with the smoke of battle, the wounded crawling with feeble limbs from the fury of the devouring flames, all seemed possessed with a common impulse. One long, unbroken cheer, in which the feeble cry of those who lay helpless on the earth, blended with the strong voices of those who still fought, rose high above the roar of battle, and hailed the presence of the victorious chief. He sat in the full realization of all that soldiers dream of—triumph; and as I looked upon him, in the complete fruition of the success which his genius, courage and confidence in his army had won, I thought that it must have been from such a scene that men in ancient time rose to the dignity of gods."

It was a brief moment of triumph for a man whose whole thought was of his cause and his country, not of his fame. Almost before the cheers died away around the Chancellor House, Lee received a note in which Jackson reported what had happened. From the officer who brought the paper Lee learned that the General had rallied from an operation for the removal of the shattered left arm. There was every reason to hope that "Stonewall" would recover, but as Lee had said to Wilbourn during the night, even the temporary loss of "Stonewall" was grievous at so critical an hour. Lee wrote Jackson: "Could I have directed events, I would have chosen for the good of the country to be disabled in your stead. I congratulate you upon the victory, which is due to your skill and energy."

Bad news was followed by worse. While Lee was preparing to renew the attack on Hooker, he heard that the Federals during the morning had attacked General Early at Fredericksburg, had driven him from the heights and probably were pursuing him toward the rear of Lee's Army. Lee had to halt the attack on Hooker and send part of his troops back to strengthen Early in beating Sedgwick.

This was not done as swiftly or as well as Lee had hoped, though some of the officers and men behaved magnificently. Perhaps the finest single accomplishment was that of Brig. Gen. Cadmus Wilcox. He had been left at a ford with instructions to stay there as long as the Federals were on the opposite bank, but to move to support Lee as soon as the Federals withdrew. Wilcox watched the enemy with ceaseless vigilance. On the morning of May 3 he observed that the Federal sentinels had over their shoulders the bags (haversacks) in which they always carried their rations. This would not have been done that day, Wilcox reasoned, unless the Federals were preparing to move off. If the sentinels had been expecting to eat at their camps, they would not have their haversacks. Wilcox based action on sound observation.

He immediately got his own troops ready for departure and late that day, by using his men quickly, he probably prevented a dangerous advance by Sedgwick.

In dealing with the Federal column from Fredericksburg, General Early also was skillful and observant, but the men were beginning to get tired. Some of the leaders were confused when they undertook to attack Sedgwick. He retreated back across the river on the night of May 4–5. By the time Lee had his troops in the Wilderness again, ready to renew the battle there, Hooker had enough. He, too, slipped back across the Rappahannock and robbed Lee of a complete victory. What had been accomplished in dealing with Hooker was enough, of course, to add greatly to the fame of the army and its commanders, but the price was excessive. Lee had lost 13,156 men, though the number killed outright was slightly less than 1,700, a small percentage of the whole. Federal losses, in comparison, were 16,845.

If Lee's losses could have been 13,155 instead of 13,156, and the subtraction of one had been a certain individual wounded on the night of May 2, the course of American history might have been different. "Stonewall" Jackson continued to improve for a day or two after the operation, but he was in a field hospital which was located where the enemy might raid it. Lee felt there was danger of the capture of Jackson and he directed that the wounded General be removed, if possible, to a place of safety. Jackson decided to go temporarily to Duiney's Station, the place where he had welcomed Mrs. Jackson and the baby when they came to visit him in April. He made the long journey in an ambulance and without apparent fatigue, but on the 7th of May he developed pneumonia. By the time Mrs. Jackson arrived, later that day, he was in a fog of fever and half-delirium.

Lee had been hopeful of Jackson's recovery. On the 6th he sent Jackson his "affectionate regards" and had urged him to "come back as soon as he can." Lee added: "He has lost his left arm, but I have lost my right arm." When Lee heard that Jackson was worse, he scarcely could believe it. He said in a shaken voice: "Surely, General Jackson must recover. God will not take him from us, now that we need him so much. Surely he will be spared to us, in answer to the many prayers which are offered for him." They were the prayers of the entire South, and not of the grief-stricken commander only. For a time the prayers seemed to avail. Jackson remained on the border line between life and death and at intervals of consciousness spoke of recovery. It was not to be. Sunday, May 10, he babbled of battles and charges and victories and then, quietly and distinctly, he said, "Let us pass over the river, and rest under the shade of the trees." That was the end.

CHAPTER THIRTEEN

Lee Loses His Greatest Battle

"I KNOW NOT how to replace him," Lee told his wife in the letter that informed her of the death of Jackson. Earnestly Lee prayed that God would raise up someone to take Jackson's place. Fervently Lee wrote John B. Hood: "We must all do more than formerly. We must endeavor to follow the unselfish, devoted, intrepid course [Jackson] pursued and we shall be strengthened rather than weakened by his loss."

Two men were thought to have equal right to consideration as Jackson's successor. One of these was A. P. Hill. He had not been on good terms with Jackson, but he had fought in Jackson's Second Corps and he commanded the division that was considered, all in all, the best in the army. The other General who seemed to fulfil many of the requirements was Richard S. Ewell. He was a man of curious appearance and odd speech. He had a bald head, a beak-like nose and something of the look of a plucked bird. When he spoke his friends said he chirped. They laughed at him but they knew him as a chivalrous, truthful gentleman, who had been the most conspicuous of Jackson's division commanders during the Valley campaign of 1862. Although Ewell had lost a leg in the Second Manassas Campaign and had not returned to the army, he was nearly well. Many believed that his former association with Jackson would help to keep alive the spirit of "Stonewall." Lee did not know Ewell well, because Ewell had not fought under him for any length of time, but Lee shared the feeling that the spirit of the

"Army of the Valley" must be preserved and that Ewell might be the man to do it.

The decision was to divide the army into three Corps, in the place of two, and to promote both A. P. Hill and Ewell to the rank of Lieutenant General. This seemed to be fair to both men and desirable for the army. As large a corps as that which Longstreet or Jackson had commanded in the spring of 1863 might include more men than a General of less experience could handle in the wooded country where the army operated.

The embarrassing fact, not realized at the time, was that Lee had to make this reorganization of the army while he was planning to enter the enemy's country for the second time. It would have been better, no doubt, if Ewell and Hill had been given time in which to accustom themselves to leading so large a force before they had to take it into battle. Events would not wait on the training of new leaders. Many things combined to make the invasion of the North more desirable in June than it could be in July. Almost as soon, therefore, as the three Corps were established, Lee started most of his army for the Shenandoah Valley and then for Maryland and Pennsylvania. He believed that Hooker would follow quickly and would try to keep between the Confederates and Washington. Until Lee was sure of this, he left A. P. Hill at Fredericksburg to watch Hooker's movements.

The first stage of the advance made the cavalry conspicuous in events about which the army talked for a long time. "Jeb" Stuart delighted in parades and reviews and all the pomp of war, and as he now had a larger force than ever he had commanded, he wanted General Lee and the other leaders to see in what fine condition the mounted troops were. Stuart consequently held a great review in Culpeper County not far from a place that bore the odd name of Brandy Station. At the close of this review, Stuart had a sham battle. His cavalry charged his artillery, which was placed close to the hill where the spectacle was being watched by a great many ladies. Those who were young and fashionable were supposed to be sensitive and delicate and were expected to faint in moments of excitement or emotion. When the cavalry galloped by, yelling and waving their sabres, many young ladies obligingly fainted but it was noticed that all those who did so had handsome male companions at hand to catch them as they fell. Strangely enough, none of the girls who were attended by unattractive men swooned.

General Lee could not attend this review, but Stuart was not to be outdone. He held another for the General. This was more businesslike and did not include any charges or mass fainting. The day after this second review, Stuart was attacked near Brandy Station by the Federal cavalry and barely was able to beat them off. This much disappointed the Southern people. Some of them confused the social review and the military review and said that if Stuart had not spent his time riding before ladies and dancing with them at night, he would not have been caught napping. Sharp criticism of Stuart appeared in newspapers. As "Jeb" greatly loved praise he felt humiliated and doubtless determined that he would do something to show his critics that he was a better fighting man than they took him to be.

This Battle of Brandy Station (or Fleetwood Hill) occurred on the 9th of June. The next morning the infantry resumed the march toward Maryland and Pennsylvania. Stuart's Cavalry remained East of the Blue Ridge so that they could keep the Federals from interfering with the swift advance. On the way northward, Ewell fiercely attacked the Federals at Winchester and captured most of their guns and the greater part of the garrison. He appeared to be as swift, as decisive and as vigorous as Jackson could have been.

As soon as Ewell and Longstreet struck their stride, Hooker left the

Rappahannock, precisely as Lee had expected, and got between the advancing Southerners and the Federal capital. Hill hastened to overtake the other troops. Everything went finely for several days. The Confederates lost contact with Hooker and did not know precisely where he was, but they reasoned that he did not know where they were either. They could keep ahead of him and soon could cross the Potomac.

When they reached the river there was less cheering and band music than there had been in September, 1862, but there were two or three incidents to make men laugh or cheer. One occurred just as the men of the First Corps were wading through the river. They had taken off their trousers, of course, as well as their shoes and were carrying their garments and footgear on their shoulders when, in the very middle of the Potomac, they met a number of carriages in which young ladies and their mamas were going to the Virginia shore on a round of visits. Many were the blushes and averted looks, but, as one soldier remarked, the spectacle was notable: "Fifty-thousand men without their trousers on can't be passed in review every day of the week."

An amusing exchange of words took place after the army had entered Pennsylvania and was passing through Chambersburg. Hundreds of civilians lined the streets and peered, of course, at General Lee. "What a large neck he has," one observer said to his neighbor. "Yes," broke in a Confederate who overheard the remark, "it takes a damn big neck to hold his head."

These onlookers, of course, had no smiles for the Confederates. None was expected beyond the borders of Maryland. "Some of the natives," a humor-loving Confederate wrote afterward, "would look very sour at us, when we would ask them for their names so we could write them on a piece of paper, so we told them, and put it in water as we knew it would turn to vinegar."

Cherries were ripe; food was more abundant; the stores were stocked with goods the Southerners bought with their own Confederate money; Ewell was far ahead of the other Corps and already was threatening Harrisburg. Everything still was prospering as late as the 28th of June, except for one disturbing fact: Lee had heard nothing for several days from "Jeb" Stuart. Before leaving Virginia, the commanding General had told Stuart to cross the Potomac where he saw fit, provided certain conditions existed. Once in Maryland and Pennsylvania, Stuart was to collect supplies and was to get in touch with Ewell. These orders had been given Stuart on the 22nd and 23rd of June. Perhaps one dispatch, written in Virginia, had been received from him. Then he had disappeared and had sent no messages. As a result, Lee did not know where the cavalry had marched. This was serious. Stuart and his men were "the eyes of the army" in locating the position and the movements of the Federals. Without reports from the cavalry commander, Lee was in the dark.

Besides the absent cavalry, the army used civilian spies to watch the enemy and to report what was happening to Northern cities and along the railroads. Most of these spies were thought to give the enemy as much information as they brought from him and they were distrusted accordingly. Longstreet had one spy of whom he had a better opinion. This was Harrison, a man in his thirties, about five feet eight inches in height, bearded, stoop-shouldered, dark and wiry. Little was known of Harrison's past, which at one time had included some experience as an actor. His reports in any event were frequent and usually were accurate. The spy spent most of his time in Washington and reported principally on what he heard and saw there.

On the night of June 28, when Lee and Longstreet were encamped with their troops at Chambersburg, Harrison put in his appearance. He had sensational news: The Army of the Potomac had crossed the

Potomac and was on the move toward Lee. Two Corps of the Army, said Harrison, were near Frederick, Maryland; two others were close to South Mountain. The troops, he added, no longer were commanded by General Hooker but were under Maj. Gen. George Gordon Meade, whom Lee knew well.

Small as was Lee's faith in spies, he realized that the moves described by Harrison were logical and therefore probable. To meet the advancing enemy, the Confederate Army must be united at once and must be moved East of the mountains. This would involve the recall of Ewell from the vicinity of Harrisburg and it would subject the entire army to danger in the absence of Stuart. Important as it was to have him in front to watch the enemy, the Confederates could not wait for him. The Army must start as soon as possible so that it could keep Meade East of the mountains and away from the roads that led to Virginia. Further, if the army must march eastward, it should strike for a town named Gettysburg. The place itself was not of great importance, but it was the hub of a large number of roads, easy to reach and an excellent starting-point for an advance in almost any direction.

Recall of Ewell from Harrisburg disappointed that officer immensely, because he had hoped to reach the Pennsylvania capital and to destroy the railroad bridges across the Susquehanna. Ewell was troubled, also, because a part of his troops were separated from him or "detached," as soldiers would say. General Early with one division had marched by way of Gettysburg to York and to Wrightsville. If Early's business had not been that of hideous war, his mission would have been full of humor and of excitement. On his way through the country around Gettysburg, for instance, he had noticed that many of the farmers had come out to the road and had made strange signs to the passing troops. Early had asked what this meant and had learned to his amusement that some rascal had been through the district ahead of the Confederates and had told the farmers that if they paid him a stiff sum, he would give them the secret sign of Southern sympathizers. When this was communicated to the passing troops, he said, the farm would not be molested. Many had paid him and were employing the "sign."

Another amusing experience befell Early in the town of York, Pennsylvania. He had in his Division an elderly political General, Ex-Governor William Smith of Virginia, a man who loved to make speeches and did so with more success than usually attends the efforts of those who like to hear themselves talk. On entering York at the head of Early's column, Smith sent back for "those tooting fellows," as he called his bandmen. He had them play "Dixie" and then "Yankee Doodle" and, as he rode on, he bowed to right and left with great politeness. Behind Smith's Brigade, Early soon observed that the column halted in the street. He pushed ahead to the town square to ascertain the reason and there he found Smith entertaining with his eloquence a throng of people who did not know whether to cheer or to jeer.

Still another strange experience of Early's mission was that of Gen. John B. Gordon, a young brigade commander of splendid personality. As Gordon was preparing to enter someone handed him a bouquet. In it he found a note in a feminine hand that told him exactly where to expect the enemy and in what strength and how to reach them. Evidently this information was given by some Southern woman who lived in the town. Gordon always was sorry he never knew who she was because her note was remarkably accurate. She would have made a superb spy.

It was well, when the campaign was over, that these and similar episodes could be remembered with amusement and laughter, because the rest was a story of bloodshed and bitterness and woe. The tragedy began in a commonplace manner. Brig. Gen. Johnston Pettigrew, commanding a fine Brigade of North Carolinians, had heard that some of the stores of Gettysburg had many shoes on their shelves. As scores of his men were almost barefooted, he procured permission to march to Gettysburg from Cashtown and to get the shoes. On the 30th of June he went, but as he approached the town he encountered Federal cavalry. Some of his officers said they thought they heard, also, the roll of drums as if infantry were being called into line on the other side of town. Pettigrew had no cavalry and no other supporting troops near at hand. He wisely decided that he should not attempt to go into Gettysburg. Without fight or delay, he quietly marched back to Cashtown and reported what happened.

If "Jeb" Stuart had been in front of the army, as he usually was, he could have taken his men over to Gettysburg and soon could have ascertained how many cavalry were there and whether they had any infantry to help them. In Stuart's absence, all that could be done by the Confederates was to guess. They guessed that only mounted troops were at Gettysburg. It would be safe, they thought, for Pettigrew's chief, Maj. Gen. Harry Heth, to march to Gettysburg the next day, to get the shoes and to drive off the Union cavalry.

This was most acceptable to Heth. He knew the soldiers needed shoes and he had discovered that Pennsylvania merchants had excellent merchandise. When he had reached Chambersburg, he had gone in search of a hat to replace the battered one he was wearing. He found that the Confederate Quartermaster already had seized all the hats in town, but he was told he might have his pick of them. He found one that suited his taste but it was too large. At the suggestion of a headquarters clerk, several sheets of paper were put under the sweat band. Heth then could wear the hat with comfort and with corresponding pleasure. He would be happy if Pettigrew's shoeless men got footgear as good as his headpiece.

The next morning, July 1, 1863, Heth started with his Division for Gettysburg. Nothing happened on the road from Cashtown until Heth in his new hat approached Willoughby Run. This stream lies on the western side of Seminary Ridge, which is high ground that overlooks the town to the East. As soon as the leading Confederate Brigades reached the Run, they encountered heavy rifle fire. Federal infantry had marched out to meet them and now gave the Southerners a hot welcome. Stiff fighting was in progress when General Lee arrived. He wanted to avoid a general battle, if he could, until all his troops were on the ground, but he found this difficult to do. The Federals were full of fight. After a time, Heth's men attacked again. Another division of Hill's arrived and made ready for battle.

Heth was barely holding his own, if he was not getting the worst of it, when the Confederates noticed that the Northerners were beginning to shift their line toward the North. Soon the reason was apparent. Ewell, in obedience to orders, was arriving from the vicinity of Harrisburg. His men and those of Hill, catching the Federals between them, swept the ridge and took about 5,000 prisoners. The price was heavy but the victory was clean cut. For Heth, the battle seemed to hold double good fortune. His men had covered themselves with honor. What was more personal, a Federal rifle ball had struck squarely the band of his new hat, but instead of entering his brain it had spent itself in the sheets of paper he had put under the band to assure himself a fit. He was badly shaken and he would not be able to exercise command for several days, but he undoubtedly was saved by that folded paper.

Lee observed most of the fight in which Ewell arrived so opportunely and Heth so narrowly escaped death. From the scene of victory, Lee rode to the crest of Seminary Ridge and looked through the afternoon sun at the scene before him. Directly ahead lay the homes and churches of Gettysburg. South of the town was a hill on which there was a cemetery. Beyond Cemetery Hill, to the East, was other high ground. Southward a long ridge extended for more than two miles and a half and ended in two rocky, round-top hills. Taken together, the elevated ground had the form of a gigantic fish-hook. The Round Tops were the eye and Cemetery Ridge was the shank of the hook, which turned toward the East at Cemetery Hill and ended in a point at an eminence which Lee was told later the natives called Culp's Hill.

As Lee watched, he could see beaten Federals in large numbers making their way to Cemetery Hill where some Union infantry and artillery were posted. Anyone could reason instantly that if the Confederates followed quickly, before the fleeing bluecoats could rally, the strong hill could be captured. Lee hoped that this would be done, but he knew how tired Hill's troops were. If Cemetery Hill could be captured at all that afternoon, Ewell's men must do it. Lee consequently sent an officer to describe to Ewell what he saw and to say that if it were practicable to seize the hill, he hoped Ewell would occupy it. Ewell did not try. He had been accustomed to fight under Jackson who always said, "Do this" or "Don't do that." When Ewell was told to use his own judgment, under the eye of the commanding General, something happened to him. He could not make up his mind what to do, though he would have obeyed any positive orders.

The result of Ewell's indecision was loss of opportunity to take the high ground that overlooked most of the country around Gettysburg. Lee had to plan something else. After talking with several of his officers, he decided that the best thing to do on the 2nd day of July would be to throw troops across the lower part of the ridge, not far North of the Round Tops, and to keep moving up the ridge until the Federals were driven from it.

In making this plan, General Lee was influenced by a curious mistake which showed how often a small thing may shape great events. On the evening of July 1, Lee had not seen any Federal troops on Cemetery Ridge, South of Cemetery Hill. None were visible in the dawn of July 2, but it was not Lee's nature to take anything for granted when the lives of his men might be lost by carelessness. Consequently, not long after daylight, he sent two of his engineers down Seminary Ridge to reconnoitre Cemetery Ridge. These officers rode southward until they were opposite the nearer eminence, which was called Little Round Top. Then they turned East to the hill and climbed part of the way up it. So far as the engineers could see, no Federals were stationed on either of the Round Tops or close to them. The engineers so reported to General Lee, who proceeded to make his plan on the assumption that no Union troops would be encountered far down the ridge. In reality, Federals had been on Little Round Top during the night and had been moved away not long before the two engineers arrived. Other troops came close to the hill about an hour later, and probably were under the hill while the engineers were on it, but they were unobserved. If the engineers had been an hour earlier or an hour later, they almost certainly would have found the bluecoats. Had General Lee known that strong hostile troops were there, he doubtless would not have attacked when or where he did. In other words, the engineers went to Little Round Top at the one time during the morning when they could have failed to see any evidence that the enemy had a great many troops on Cemetery Ridge.

General Lee had another disadvantage in attacking that day. His senior lieutenant, General James Longstreet, had won easy success at Fredericksburg in December, 1862, by waiting till the enemy came and attacked him. Longstreet believed that it would be possible to do this nearly always and he thought the effort always should be made to make the Federals assail a strong position. Before the army had gone into Pennsylvania, Longstreet had talked of this plan with Lee and had thought that the commanding General had agreed to fight the way Longstreet thought he should. Lee never had any intention of promising that. When he found the enemy at Gettysburg, he felt that the thing to do was to attack. Longstreet thought this was the wrong way of conducting the battle, and when Lee insisted, Longstreet got mad. His chief of staff wrote later: "As Longstreet was not to be made willing and Lee refused to change or could not change, the former failed to conceal some anger. There was apparent apathy in his movements. They lacked the fire and point of his usual bearing on the battlefield."

Lee's plan of action was not a good one. Longstreet's sullenness, consequent delay and the mistake about the strength of the Federals made it worse. The Confederates attacked on the afternoon of July 2 with much courage and they captured a peach orchard that was a fine position for artillery, but they could not drive the Federals from the ridge. When the struggle of the day ended, General Lee felt that he had to make a final effort to drive the Federals from the ridge and to defeat them. He believed that if he put strong artillery in the peach orchard and got all his troops to work together, he could win.

The 3rd of July was a clear day, warm but not uncomfortably hot. A pleasant west wind was blowing. Pickett's fine Virginia troops, who belonged to Longstreet's Corps, were chosen to lead the principal charge. They had not previously been in the battle at Gettysburg and they were in fighting trim. Lee wanted the other troops of Longstreet's Corps to share the charge, but when Longstreet argued against this, Lee decided to use Heth's Division. Included in this Division, which belonged to Hill's Corps, were many North Carolinians. They had full faith in their leader, Gen. Johnston Pettigrew, who acted in place of the wounded Heth.

Both Pickett and Pettigrew were told to keep their men West of the crest of Seminary Ridge, away from the enemy's fire and where the soldiers could not see the wide field of 1,400 yards across which they were to charge. The men were not deceived by this. They guessed what they were to be required to do and they made ready with their usual combination of humor and seriousness. Shortly after 1 o'clock, they heard the signal guns fired on the eastern side of the ridge. In a few seconds, the ridge shook with the pulsing of the bombardment that was to precede their attack. A shell from a long-range gun exploded among the bushes and sent a rabbit scampering to the rear. One Confederate cried after the animal, "Run, old hahr; if I was an old hahr I would run too." The men laughed, of course, but presently they knelt silently and bare-headed while the chaplains offered prayer.

"This is a desperate thing to attempt," said General Richard Garnett to General Lewis Armistead, who, like himself, commanded a Brigade of Pickett's Division.

"It is," Armistead answered, "but the issue is with the Almighty, and we must leave it in His hands."

On the ridge, at a point from which he could see the whole line as it advanced, Lee was waiting. Not far away Longstreet was wrestling with his own lack of faith in the success of the charge. When Pickett rode up, he asked, "General, shall I advance?" Longstreet could not bring himself to answer but at last he bowed his head by way of silent assent. Pickett saluted. "I am going to move forward, sir," he said, and galloped off.

As soon as Pickett reached his men, he called them: "Up, men, and to your posts! Don't forget today that you are from old Virginia." Farther up the line, Pettigrew appealed in like spirit to one of his stout-hearted officers: "Now, Colonel, for the honor of the good Old North State, forward."

"Sergeant," cried Armistead to the color-bearer, "are you going to put those colors on the enemy's works today?"

"I will try, sir," came the answer, "and if mortal man can do it, it shall be done."

Armistead took off his hat, stuck it on the point of his sword, lifted the blade high over his head where all could see it and cried in his clear voice: "Attention, Second Battalion, the battalion of direction. Forward, guide center! March!"

Out into the open moved the long, long line. Clear of the woods, it was halted. Officers straightened it as carefully as if the troops were on dress parade. Nineteen battleflags were flying; the roar of the Southern guns was a shout of defiance. Then, on command, the men began to move down the low ridge to a shallow meadow and across it toward the fences on the stone-covered ridge. The objective was a little grove of trees, high on Cemetery Ridge, where Federal guns had been belching death.

Over the field, into the range of the Union artillery and then onward till they could hear the whine of rifle bullets, the Southerners moved. Soon they were stumbling and falling dead or crying out in anguish when wounded. On the extreme left, where the Confederates had only one line, they began to waver. Lee watched them through his glasses and saw that some of the soldiers were dropping back. The others pressed on until the whole line disappeared at the foot of Cemetery Ridge in dust and smoke. For a few minutes the rebel yell could be heard above the fire of thousands of rifles and scores of cannon. Then the rattle of musketry was a little less loud. Presently it began to die away as if there were no more men to be killed. Here and there the smoke lifted. Through it, presently, back toward the Confederate lines, the survivors of the charge began to stream. Smoke-covered or bleeding, defiant or weeping, pushing onward or looking backward to fire or to scream defiance, the men of Pickett and of Pettigrew made their way. The charge had failed. They had attempted the impossible.

Out among them Lee rode to rally and to cheer them. "All will come right in the end," he told them; "we'll talk it over afterwards—we want all good and true men just now." Soon he saw Pickett and spurred to him. "General Pickett," he said, "place your Division in rear of this hill, and be ready to repel the advance of the enemy should they follow up their advantage."

Pickett was frantic. "General Lee," he cried, "I have no division now, Armistead is down, Garnett is down, and Kemper is mortally wounded."

"Come, General Pickett," Lee answered, "this has been my fight and upon my shoulders rests the blame." He went on warmly: "The men and officers of your command have written the name of Virginia as high today as it has ever been written before."

In the same spirit he spoke to a wounded leader and later to Cadmus Wilcox, who sought vainly to explain how his famous brigade had been shattered. "Never mind, General," Lee replied, "all this has been my fault— it is *I* that have lost this fight, and you must help me out of it the best way you can."

Lee found himself now among some prisoners who had been captured earlier in the day. One of these was a wounded boy who cried patriotically when he saw the General ride past, "Hurrah for the Union!" Lee drew rein and then wheeled toward the spot where the boy was lying. The Union soldier caught his breath because he thought the unknown Southerner on the horse was riding over to put a bullet through his head. Lee dismounted and extended his hand. "My son," he said, "I hope you will soon be well."

Late in the evening, after he had heard that Ewell as well as Longstreet had failed to drive the enemy, Lee went wearily back to his camp. "General," said one of his officers, "this has been a hard day on you."

"Yes, it has been a sad, sad day for us." He paused, reflected and then broke out: "I never saw troops behave more magnificently than Pickett's Division of Virginians did today in that grand charge upon the enemy. And if they had been supported as they were to have been— but for some reason not yet fully explained to me, were not—we would have held that position and the day would have been ours." Again he paused and added, "Too bad, too bad! Oh, too bad!"

He held his ground a day, as he had after the Battle of Sharpsburg, and then, through a heavy rain, on the evening of July 4, he started his wagon-trains for the Potomac. With their groaning loads of wounded and with bewildered men all around, the wagons were pulled over the mountains. As the army retreated, Lee might have said in perfect justice that he was misled into battle in the absence of "Jeb" Stuart, who had not returned until the afternoon of July 2nd from a raid that had been prolonged to no good purpose when the cavalry should have been covering the infantry advance. With equal truth Lee could have said that Ewell had been unable to decide anything on the first day of the battle and afterward had achieved little in a succession of costly attacks. Longstreet might have been blamed along with Stuart and Ewell. Lee could have said that the reorganized army had been spread over so much ground that it could not develop teamwork. It probably never occurred to Lee to say any of this or to undertake to shirk responsibility for what had happened to the army he commanded. As its leader, he was to blame. He would not attempt to put on other shoulders the load he felt was rightly his. On the night of the 4th of July, when he came to the camp fire at Longstreet's bivouac, he said clearly, perhaps that others beside Longstreet might hear, "It's all my fault. I thought my men were invincible."

CHAPTER FOURTEEN

Lee Endures a Hard Winter

FORTUNATELY FOR LEE, he was not pursued swiftly from Gettysburg. He was able to reach the Potomac River and, after a delay on account of high water, to bring his troops back to Virginia soil. It was a sad return. In Pennsylvania the Confederates had lost 23,000 killed, wounded and prisoners. Federal casualties were about the same, but were not so serious because Meade's fallen could be replaced. Lee's could not be. His army was never as strong again as when he entered Pennsylvania.

Because he felt he had failed at Gettysburg, Lee asked President Davis to relieve him of command and to put in his place, as he said, "a younger and abler man." The President of course declined to do this and expressed his entire confidence in Lee's direction of the army. Obedient to duty and to lawful authority, the General then undertook the hard, slow task of rebuilding his weakened forces.

For a time in September, Lee was still weaker, rather than stronger, because Longstreet and two of his divisions were sent to Tennessee to join Gen. Braxton Bragg in an attack on the Federals under Gen. W. S. Rosecrans. Soon afterward, the Federals, too, transferred troops to Tennessee. This partially restored the balance between Union and Southern troops in Virginia and prompted Lee to assail his foe again. In October part of the Confederate troops moved against Meade, but his line of retreat was shorter than Lee's line of pursuit. Lee did not overtake the Federals until they were near Bristoe Station, south of Manassas Junction. There A. P. Hill attacked at once, but in his zeal he did not take time to examine carefully the Federal position. The result was that he overtook thousands of Union soldiers who were hidden in a railroad cut. A fierce fire by these bluecoats almost destroyed two North Carolina Brigades.

The day after this battle of October 14 at Bristoe Station, Lee went over the field with A. P. Hill, who tried to explain what had happened. With few words of his own, Lee listened and then remarked grimly, "Well, well, General, bury these poor men and let us say no more about it." By that he meant that nothing could be said to justify Hill's hasty attack. Nothing was to be gained, either, by following Meade's Army to the defences of Washington. The Confederates reversed their march and went back to the south bank of the Rappahannock River where it had been crossed by the burned bridge of the Orange and Alexandria, now the Southern Railway.

The advance had accomplished no good and had inflicted many hardships on soldiers who did not have shoes. Two things saved the march from being an operation on which the men looked back with unrelieved sadness. The speed of the march to Bristoe had itself been humorous. Brigades never had moved so fast. When the reason was discovered, everyone had to laugh: The soldiers had hurried because many of them remembered how in the summer of 1862 they had marched to Bristoe and then to Manassas Junction where they had feasted on stores the Federals had accumulated there. They had raced top speed to Bristoe on their second visit in the hope that they might have equally good luck.

The Confederate cavalry had the other amusing adventure. In moving toward Bristoe to cover the infantry's advance, Stuart and part of his men were cut off at Auburn, near Warrenton, Fauquier County.

In the belief that the enemy were on three sides of his column of mounted men, Stuart hid his troops in a field and stayed there all night. Orders were stern that the soldiers must not make any move to indicate their presence. The men were as quiet as Stuart could have asked them to be, but the hungry mules that pulled the wagons did not understand the need of silence. Every now and then one of them would hee-haw loudly. Stuart had finally to station a man at the head of each animal to stifle every bray. The next morning about dawn, as the Southerners looked out from their hiding place, they could see the Federals making and drinking coffee by the roadside. The Confederates became so hungry for the coffee that they thought they could smell the drink. When at last they were ready to dash off, after daylight, they had great satisfaction in turning their artillery on the coffee pots and the frying pans, which they knocked high in the air.

Back on the Rappahannock River, Lee had on November 7 an experience that was unrelieved by humor. Parts of two Brigades on the north side of the river, occupying what was called a "fortified bridgehead," were captured just before nightfall. This disaster made it necessary to burn immediately the pontoon bridges the Confederates had thrown across the river. A young soldier named William Effinger volunteered to start the fire, though everyone assumed that the Union sharpshooters on the opposite side would "pick him off" the moment he struck a light. In defiance of this risk, Effinger went to the end of the bridge, started the fire and nursed it until it was blazing furiously. Like Sergeant Richard Kirkland at Fredericksburg, he did not receive a single shot!

After this affair of the Rappahannock Bridge, Lee regretfully had to move back to the Rapidan the soldiers who had made themselves comfortable on the Rappahannock. The men knew that he would not have changed their winter quarters if he had not been compelled to do so, and when they established themselves on the Rapidan, they proceeded to cut down logs and to construct huts, or else they built chimneys to their tents.

Few of the troops had so pleasant a winter as the previous one near Fredericksburg. Late in November, the men had to leave their camps and hurry down the river to Mine Run, where Meade had advanced the Federal Army. The bluecoats did not remain many days on Mine Run before they recrossed the Rapidan, without a battle, but the weather was so severe that the thin-clad Southerners could not have endured it if they had not become accustomed to an out-of-door life.

Along with lack of warm clothing, the men had to face a tragic shortage of food. When the railways failed to deliver supplies or the roads were too muddy for the wagons to reach the front, the soldiers had nothing whatever to eat. Often the rations for an entire day consisted of four ounces of bad bacon and a pint of corn meal. This scanty subsistance on corn meal, day after day, became the subject of jest. The two armies, a punster said, were the fed and the corn-fed.

General Lee suffered agonies over the hunger of the men and over the distress of the horses. Once during the winter, when food was scarcely to be had at all, Lee received a package from a private soldier. In it was the thin bit of fat meat issued the soldier that day as a ration. The anonymous sender said in an accompanying letter that he had been born a gentleman, but that gnawing hunger had compelled him to steal in order to keep alive.

Another soldier wrote to ask whether Lee knew how little food the troops actually were getting. If Lee was conscious of the shortage and was not able to overcome it, then, the soldier assured him, the men would endure it. Lee made this brave letter the occasion of an order in which he told of special conditions that kept the government from delivering food. "It is hoped," said Lee, "that the exertion now being made will render the necessity of short duration, but the history of the army has shown that the country can require no sacrifice too great for its patriotic devotion." He continued: "Soldiers! You tread with no unequal step the road by which your fathers marched through suffering, privations, and blood to independence. Continue to emulate in the future, as you have in the past, their valor in arms, their patient endurance of hardships, their high resolve to be free, which no trial could shake, no bribe seduce, no danger appal, and be assured that the just God who crowned their efforts with success will, in His own good time, send down His blessing upon yours."

A General who spoke in that spirit to the men in his care was certain to have not only their respect but also their affection and their admiration. Lee in his modesty never realized how devoted to him his soldiers were. One day, for example, as he was directing a battle, Lee saw a boy going slowly to the rear with a shattered right arm. "I grieve for you, my poor fellow," said Lee. "Can I do anything for you?"

"Yes, sir; you can shake hands with me, General, if you will consent to take my left hand." Lee almost wept as he shook the soldier's hand.

During the winter, some of the men were discussing around a camp fire Charles Darwin's *Origin of Species,* a recently-published book in which the doctrine of evolution was expounded clearly for the first time. The soldiers did not know the distinctions Darwin drew. All they had was the popular idea that Darwin proclaimed that "man was descended from a monkey." This the men were debating. A surprising number of them accepted the theory, but one of the group was unyielding. "Well, boys," he said, "the rest of us may have developed from monkeys; but I tell you none less than God could have made such a man as 'Marse Robert.' " That ended the argument.

Slowly in such debates as this, and in unhesitating faith in the wisdom of their leader, the men passed the icy months of unrelenting winter. Few of the soldiers knew General Lee had a burden of personal care in addition to the load he bore for his country and his troops. Mrs. Lee had become an invalid from arthritis and no longer could walk; one of the General's sons was a prisoner of war; while this son was at the mercy of the jailer, the young man's wife died; Lee continued to grieve for his daughter Annie who had died in October, 1862; another daughter had the distress of reading that a rejected suitor of hers had been hanged by the Federals as a Confederate spy.

To all this sorrow was added the loss of Arlington. The Federal Congress had imposed a direct tax on all property owned within the Union lines by Confederates. To make certain that the property could be confiscated for non-payment of taxes, officials required that all Confederates must pay their taxes in person. If a Confederate had appeared to pay the levy, he would have been arrested and imprisoned. A kinsman of General Lee offered the sum due on Arlington but it was refused. The place then was sold for delinquent taxes. This confiscation was brought up in an interview with Lee by an Austrian officer who was visiting headquarters in a part of Virginia that had been stripped of all its food and all its live stock. Lee did not complain because of what had been done about Arlington. "That," Lee told the Austrian, "I can easily understand, and for that I don't care; but I do feel sorry for the poor creatures I see here, starved and driven from their homes for no reason whatsoever."

This and all his sorrow Lee bore in silence but in constant prayer to the God whose hand he sought to acknowledge in all things. Through Northern newspapers he learned of new preparations for the campaign of 1864. General Ulysses S. Grant had assumed command of all the land forces of the United States and had decided to maintain his headquarters with Meade's Army so that he could advise Meade in fighting Lee. The first news of this new association of two of the ablest of

Union Generals reached Lee at a time when he had been suffering from pains in the chest and shoulder. "Colonel," he said to one of his staff officers, "we have to whip them; we must whip them, and it has already made me better to think of it."

Lee at that time was doing everything he could to increase the size of his army. He was hoping for the early return from Tennessee of General Longstreet, who had experienced much unhappiness and small success while absent from Virginia. All other troops who could be spared from the Carolinas and from Tennessee, Lee was anxious to bring to the Rapidan.

When Longstreet's two Divisions actually arrived, late in April, Lee went to see the old veterans of the First Corps. They had polished their arms and greased their shoes and patched their uniforms to make a decent appearance when he reviewed them. Said one of Longstreet's soldiers: "General Lee must have felt good in getting the welcome extended to him by those who had been lost to him so long. The men hung around him and seemed satisfied to lay their hands on his gray horse or to touch the bridle, or the stirrup, or the old General's leg— anything that Lee had was sacred to us fellows who had just come back. And the General—he could not help from breaking down . . . tears traced down his cheeks, and he felt that we were again to do his bidding."

Confident as Lee was of the experience, the valor and the devotion of his soldiers, he knew, also, that the odds against him were heavier than ever they had been. His machine of war was beginning to wear out. That of the Federals had been repaired where weak and had been renewed where shaken. The Army of the Potomac was stronger, better disciplined and better led than ever it had been. Daily the scouts told of indications of an early Federal advance. Spies brought back word that a large force was assembling around Annapolis presumably to cooperate with Grant. When the trees began to leaf and the spring grass was high enough to give some feed to the horses, Grant would strike. By the 2nd of May, it was certain that the opening of a great offensive by the Federals was a matter of a few days only. Lee watched, made ready, counselled his Generals, and wrote to his son: "Our country demands all our strength, all our energies. To resist the powerful combination now forming against us will require everyman at his place. If victorious, we have everything to hope for in the future. If defeated, nothing will be left for us to live for. . . . My whole trust is in God, and I am ready for whatever he may ordain."

CHAPTER FIFTEEN

Two Weeks of Battle

GRANT'S BLOW FELL on the 4th of May, 1864, when the great Federal Army crossed the Rappahannock and plunged into the Wilderness. To meet this advance, Lee moved the Army of Northern Virginia down the Rapidan. He did not undertake to fight directly on the bank of the river, because he thought he could do the greatest damage to the Federals while they were marching through the tangle of the Wilderness. Grant was much pleased at getting across the river. He had believed that would be his hardest task. Once in the Wilderness, he thought he could fight his way out of it.

The Battle of the Wilderness began as soon as the opposing troops met on the 5th of May. Lee had told his men to attack. Grant's orders were to the same effect. The clash was fierce. Near the river, where the Confederates first struck the bluecoats, the end of the day's hard struggle found the two armies far enough apart for a soldier to know when he was "off side." At twilight on the other flank, Federals and Confederates were so close together in the woods that if a man left his company and went to look for water, he was apt to walk into the opposing line and be made prisoner.

This happened frequently on the Plank road, which ran eastward to Fredericksburg. The two Confederate Generals who had charge of the troops on that road asked A. P. Hill to let them untangle the lines, but he refused. He did not intend, he said, to disturb the tired men.

Longstreet's Corps, Hill explained, was coming forward that night and would take over the lines.

At daylight the next morning, General Lee rode with his staff to the Plank road. He was close to the front, on the Tapp Farm, when the Federals began a furious attack. In a few minutes the Confederates poured back down the Plank road in rapid retreat. The Union troops followed fast. Lee found that nothing stood between him and the enemy except some artillery that might be captured soon. Half-an-hour's fighting had brought a desperate crisis. If the Federals were not stopped, the Confederate Army might be thrown against the bank of the river and destroyed.

Presently, the Federals were so close to the artillery that there scarcely seemed time for the gunners to load and fire before they would have to gallop off to escape capture. The commander of the artillery took the long chance and fired another round. It held off the Unionists for a few minutes more. Lee had been looking back anxiously along the Plank road for the arrival of Longstreet's troops, and now, while the attacking Federals hesitated, he noticed that twenty men or more were coming toward him from the rear. "Who are you, my boys?" Lee called to them.

"Texas boys," they yelled back.

They did not have to say anything more. Lee understood. They belonged to Hood's famous Texas Brigade of Longstreet's Corps, which now was hurrying to the front to save Hill's retreating troops. For once, General Lee's excitement got the better of him. He jerked off his hat and waved it over his head. "Hurrah for Texas, hurrah for Texas," he cried.

Soon the Texans were numerous enough to form a line that would stop the oncoming Federals, but that was not all that would be required. The Federals must be attacked and driven back into the woods.

A charge must be delivered; Lee wanted to head it; the Texans refused to let him take that risk. "Go back, General Lee," they cried, "go back." He paid no attention to them. Some of them stopped and shouted, "We don't go on unless you go back." Still he kept ahead until a tall sergeant seized his bridle rein. Even then Lee might have insisted on joining the charge if one of his staff officers had not come up and told him that Longstreet was at hand and wished to consult him.

Reluctantly, Lee went back to talk to Longstreet, whose men at that moment were giving an example of fine discipline and courage. They had formed a line on either side of the road and were standing their ground while Hill's men passed through their ranks. The veterans of Longstreet knew that Hill's Corps would rally, but of course they had to make some fun of the soldiers who were running to the rear. "Do you belong to Lee's Army?" they yelled. "You don't look like the men we left here!"

Soon the retreat stopped. While the troops of Hill rested and dressed their wounds, Longstreet led his men forward. He quickly drove the bluecoats into the Wilderness and then he learned that if he sent troops southward through the woods, he could get on the flank of the Federals and throw them back toward the river. By swift action, the Confederates might do to the enemy what the Federals tried to do to them earlier in the day.

Lee watched Longstreet's preparations for this flank attack. Soon Lee heard from the South the swelling sound of rifle-fire as the men of the First Corps fell on the surprised Unionists. The attack was a perfect success. Gen. W. S. Hancock, the Federal commander, later admitted that the Southerners rolled up his left flank as if it had been a blanket.

Everything held the promise of glorious success when a messenger galloped up to Lee with bad news: Longstreet had been shot by some of his own troops who had mistaken him and his staff for Federals! In deepest distress, Lee started at once for the Plank road. There he found that the advance of the Confederates had been halted when Longstreet fell. Lines were tangled. Troops were confused. By the time Lee could get the situation in hand again, the Federals had rallied. An attack that might have routed them at noon was beaten off easily in the late afternoon.

Lee realized this and rode over to the other flank of his Army to see if anything could be done there. He found an amazing state of affairs. A young Georgian General, John B. Gordon, had discovered during the morning that the last of the Union troops had moved southward from the river bank and were waiting in the woods for orders to continue their march. As soldiers would say, the right flank of the Federals was "in the air," where the Confederates could attack it easily. Gordon had reported this promptly to General Ewell, who commanded all the troops on the Confederate left. Ewell trusted Gordon, but did not know what to do because General Early, the officer directly over Gordon, said that the Georgian was completely mistaken. The Union right, Early insisted, was *not* "in the air." A strong Federal force was in rear of the troops Gordon had seen. Others were nearer the river and were threatening the Confederate left. An attack would be too dangerous.

General Lee listened as all this was explained to him. He turned to General Gordon and briefly questioned that young officer. Gordon's answers convinced Lee that the Georgian was correct and that the attack should be made. Ewell was told that Gordon should go forward and must have adequate support. As soon as Lee decided that this was the thing to do, Ewell dropped his indecision and Early his opposition. Both did their utmost to help Gordon. He attacked and found the situation still was exactly as he had described it to Ewell during the forenoon. Quickly Gordon's fine Georgia troops got on the flank of the Federals and drove the Unionists before them until darkness compelled them to halt.

So ended the strange battle of the 6th of May. There never had been in the army's history as many changes of fortune in any previous day as had occurred between the opening of the attack on Hill at dawn and the halt of Gordon's counter-attack at nightfall. The Confederates had, on the whole, the better of the fighting, but they had lost many experienced officers and some thousands of good troops.

That sad fact was not all that Lee had to consider. Always, in previous campaigns, after the Federals had been pounded hard for two or three days, they had retreated. This time, they were ending their third day in the Wilderness and they gave no sign of any intention to break off the battle. If dawn of May 7 should find the Army of Grant still in position and ready to fight, Lee might have to face the prospect of a long and exhausting struggle.

The 7th of May did not bring a renewal of the battle, nor did it find the Federals in retreat, but daybreak presented a hideous picture. All night, fire had been sweeping through the Wilderness. Many trees had crashed. Others had been burned till they were bare skeletons. Long, black vistas opened through the Wilderness where the previous day a green screen had cut off vision. As the ambulance squads moved over the still-smouldering fire, they could see places where a soldier with a broken leg or a broken back had tried to make a little clearing around him while the fire had come closer and closer to him. In the end he had failed. He lay there in contortion. Heat had killed him if the flames had not actually reached him.

In that scene of desolation, Grant remained. He did not offer battle; he appeared willing to meet any attack. As Lee watched during the morning, he began to suspect that Grant was not going to stay in the

Wilderness. The Federals were preparing, Lee thought, to make another move—and not a move back to safety on the north bank of the Rappahannock. Grant either was going down the river toward Fredericksburg, or else he was planning to continue to the southeast, through the Wilderness, in order to get the railroads on which the Confederates depended for supplies. If the Unionists were making ready to march southeastward, they probably would go first to a place known as Spotsylvania Court House, where a number of roads met.

Through the day of the 7th, Lee studied all the evidence of Grant's movements exactly as a detective pieces together the evidence of a crime. Before nightfall Lee concluded that the Federals would move to Spotsylvania, rather than to Fredericksburg. To keep them from getting between him and Richmond, he decided to send part of his troops to the Court House, near which "Jeb" Stuart already had most of the Confederate cavalry. Two members of Lee's staff were directed to ride to Stuart's position and to tell him that infantry would arrive the next day to support him. One of the officers who went on that mission wrote afterward: "This faculty of General Lee, of discovering as if by intuition, the intention and purpose of his opponent, was a very remarkable one. . . . I remarked to my comrade [on the ride to Stuart] . . . that I saw no indication of a movement by Grant's army in that direction, as they appeared to be present in heavy force along our entire front; but when I reached the cavalry I found it hotly engaged with the enemy's infantry . . . and wondered at the unerring discernment of General Lee."

The assistance promised Stuart was received the next day earlier than had been expected. The reason was highly interesting. After Longstreet was wounded on the 6th, there was uncertainty whether he would die or recover. In either event, someone else would have to direct the First Corps for weeks, perhaps for months. Lee considered all the possibilities and decided that General "Dick" Anderson was best suited for the command of the Corps. Anderson accordingly was named on the 7th. One of the first orders given him was to this effect: As soon as possible after nightfall, Anderson was to withdraw his men quietly from the line and was to take them to the vicinity of a new road that had been cut southward through the woods. Not later than 3 o'clock on the morning of the 8th, Anderson was to start for Spotsylvania Court House, which was distant eleven miles.

Before Anderson withdrew from the line, he decided that 3 A.M. was too late an hour at which to begin his march. He would start for Spotsylvania at 11 P.M. so as to be on time. After he got his men from the front, he found the Wilderness so uncomfortably hot and so full of smoke that he determined not to halt and wait till 11 o'clock. He would keep moving until he was clear of the Wilderness. A grand send-off his men had. On the right of his line, someone raised the rebel yell. Every country-born boy who had chased foxes knew how to give that yell. Thousands took it up that May night. Down the whole length of the line the cry swept to the Confederate left. It was given a second time and a third—"the grandest rebel yell of the war," one Confederate insisted.

The hearts of Anderson's men beat the higher because of that yell; their pace was steady, though the road was full of stumps and fragments of tree-limbs. About 3 o'clock on the morning of the 8th, the infantry halted and ate such breakfast as they had. Then they pushed on again toward Spotsylvania.

When the leading troops reached a point about a mile and a half from the Court House, they observed an elderly gentleman riding toward them from the North at a furious pace. As he came a little closer, the soldiers saw that he was a civilian without hat or shoes. He galloped up, sought the nearest officer and told of a desperate situation:

Up the road along which he had ridden, he said, Confederate cavalry were fighting against a great mass of Federals. The Southerners had made some piles of rails, which they could use for field defences, but infantry would be needed to help the cavalry.

Anderson did not hesitate. As quickly as he could pass word, he ordered two famous old Brigades, one from South Carolina and one from Mississippi, to move at once up the road to support the cavalry. Scarcely had these Brigades started than another mounted man spurred to them. "Run for our rail piles," he shouted, "the Federal infantry will reach them first, if you don't run!" The Confederates dashed across the field, hurried behind the piles of rails, and soon had their bullets flying. This rifle-fire stopped the Federals temporarily and gave the Confederates a position from which they spread to right and to left.

All this had been a narrow escape from disaster. Unless Anderson's men had arrived, the Confederate cavalry almost certainly would have been driven from Spotsylvania Court House. If Anderson had not begun his march when he did, he could not possibly have reached the battleground in time to "save the day." The Army of the Potomac would have commanded the crossroads and would have stood between Lee and Richmond. Great had been the reward of an early start!

Additional troops of both Armies now moved steadily to Spotsylvania Court House until, by evening of the 9th, a strong, long Confederate line had been drawn there. Lee remained between Grant and the roads to Richmond, but when the Confederates began to build trenches on the best ground they could find, they had a strange experience that later cost them many lives. On the night of the 8th, the Division of Gen. Edward Johnson, of Ewell's Second Corps, was ordered to extend the line toward Spotsylvania. Johnson had no guide and consequently had to feel his way through the darkness. Soon he saw

Federal campfires ahead of him. One of Johnson's aides thus described what followed: "The ground was examined, and General Johnson found we were on the brow of a ridge, which turned somewhat shortly to the right. The camp fires in our front seemed to us to be considerably below the plane of our position, as they were in fact. It was now quite late in the night, and General Johnson deflected his line and followed the ridge so far as it could be distinguished in the darkness."

When morning came, the Confederates found that the ground occupied by Johnson had the outline of a mule shoe. The toe of it was almost a mile nearer the Federal position than the main Confederate line was. At its widest point, the shoe covered about 1,200 yards, This salient, as the Generals called it, was partly covered by forest and would be difficult to defend. If it were abandoned, it would give the Federals the advantage of high ground. General Lee consequently decided to hold the "Mule Shoe" by placing abundant artillery there along with the good troops of the stout Second Corps.

On the afternoon of the 10th of May, Union troops broke into the western side of the "Mule Shoe" but met with a prompt repulse. The next day no special threat was made to the exposed position. In fact, late that day the reports from cavalry outposts indicated that the Federals might be preparing to move again. As the few roads inside the heavily-wooded "Mule Shoe" were narrow, Lee thought it would be wise to take the artillery out before nightfall, so that, if the enemy did march off, the Confederates could follow quickly the next day. The guns in the salient were removed accordingly, and were parked in the rear.

From early afternoon of the 11th, a cold, heavy rain had been falling. The myriad leaves of the great trees inside the salient were restless and noisy under the lash of the wind. Strangely enough, all the Federal bands on the line opposite the "Mule Shoe" played while the rain pelted down. It was almost midnight when the music ceased. After that the air was filled increasingly with nervous sound. Nobody knew what was happening; everyone on guard felt that something was astir. About 2 o'clock, suspicion arose that the Federals were massing for an attack on the "Mule Shoe." Orders were sent for the artillery to return.

The gunners started back and reached the salient, but before many of them could make ready to fire, a swarm of Federals swept over the earthworks and opened what proved to be one of the bitterest day's fighting the Army of Northern Virginia ever had to endure. Nearly all of Johnson's Division was captured. General Gordon quickly collected his troops to meet the enemy, but if he were delayed or beaten, the Confederate line might be cut in half. This prospect so alarmed General Lee that he wanted to lead an immediate charge. Gordon pleaded with him not to go into the line of fire; the soldiers cried "Lee to the rear"; the General persisted until one of the men turned Traveller around in the woods.

Gordon's men courageously fought their way up the salient, yard by yard. On their left, the troops of Gen. Robert Rodes matched their valor. Other troops were thrown into the "Mule Shoe." By the most desperate fighting, the Confederates reached the "toe," but they could not drive the Federals from the outer side. The men jabbed at one another through holes between logs. Rifles were thrown over the works so that the bayonet would pin down any man it hit. So fast did some of the Confederates have to fire, that they could not take time to reach into a cartridge box. They stretched out the stiffening arms of dead comrades by their side and put their cartridges in hands that never again would pull a trigger. The Southerners at the tip of the salient were told they must stay there and hold the Federals at bay until a new trench could be dug across the rear or base of the "Mule Shoe." Obediently all day and until nearly midnight the Confederates hung on. Perhaps as many as 5,000 of them had been killed, wounded or captured when, at last, the survivors were told they could fall back.

The next day the men were amazed to see how intense the infantry fire had been. Rifle bullets alone had so riddled the trunk of a tree twenty-two inches in diameter that it had fallen with a crash. Another giant with a diameter of twenty inches had fallen in the same way. No wonder the soldiers stopped speaking of the "Mule Shoe" and styled the salient the "Bloody Angle."

It was not there alone that Lee met disaster on the 12th of May. "Jeb" Stuart and most of his cavalry had ridden off on the 9th in pursuit of the Federal mounted troops, who had undertaken a raid against Richmond and the railroads that led to the city. At Yellow Tavern about seven miles north of Richmond, Stuart had been able to put his tired men and his thin horses between the Unionists and their prize. "I must save the women and children of Richmond," Stuart had said.

In the confused fighting that followed the arrival of the Union troops, Stuart received a wound in the abdomen. As he was being carried from the field, he shouted to some of his men, "Go back, go back and do your duty as I have done mine, and your country will be safe. Go back, go back." Then he had added, "I had rather die than be whipped." News of this had reached Lee while the battle of the 12th was at full fury. Late that night he learned that Stuart had died in Richmond. "He never brought me a piece of false information," Lee said sorrowfully. To Mrs. Lee he wrote: "A more zealous, ardent, brave and devoted soldier than Stuart the Confederacy cannot have."

The death of Stuart added to the burden of command that Lee was now carrying with less help than at any time since the Seven Days. Longstreet fortunately had rallied from his wound and had good prospect of recovery; but he would be absent for months. A. P. Hill temporarily was too sick to direct the Third Corps. Ewell was so feeble that Lee was afraid he would collapse any day. Now Stuart was dead. More decisions than ever would have to be made by the commanding General. He had to plan and to execute, too.

In order to discharge all the duties now demanded of him, Lee rose at 3 A.M. and often worked until late at night. His staff officers could see that he was under heavy physical strain and in danger of illness, but they had greater admiration for him than ever as they saw how sternly he kept his self-control and held to his code of courtesy and kindness. One day a tired artillerist came to headquarters with a message for the General. Lee saw that the young officer was weary and he doubtless reflected that his guest was hungry, also. There was no food to offer, but Lee addressed the officer as if he had been at Arlington in the ample days of ease. "Captain," said he, "may I bring you a drink of water?" The officer of whom that question was asked, W. Gordon McCabe, became in time a famous teacher of boys and a friend of many renowned men, but he never could tell without tears that little story of Lee's courtesy.

More dramatic were Lee's answers to some of the wrathful utterances of his lieutenants. On reconnaissance one day, he heard a high-ranking Confederate express the wish that all the Federals were dead and in hell. Lee asked, "How can you say that, General?" and he added simply: "Now, I wish they were all at home attending to their own business, and leaving us to do the same." He never referred to the Federals as "Yankees" and seldom called them "the enemy" unless he was much excited. Usually he referred to them as "those people." He said after the war that he had never failed during the whole of the conflict to pray for them.

General Lee saw to it, also, that those Union soldiers who fell into his hands received as much food and had as much care as his army could provide. In front of Spotsylvania, during the cavalry raid on

Richmond, one Confederate General who was somewhat notorious for taking the best possible care of himself began to rebuke Stuart's men for permitting the Federals to destroy the reserve rations of the army in the raid already mentioned. The complaining General continued: "And they have captured my cow, and I have no milk for my coffee. If I were in command of this army, I would notify General Grant that, inasmuch as he had sent his cavalry to the rear and destroyed our rations, I would not give his prisoners whom we hold a morsel of food, and if he wanted to save them from starvation, he would have to send rations here to them."

Lee broke out: "The prisoners that we have here, General, are my prisoners; they are not General Grant's prisoners, and as long as I have any rations at all I shall divide them with *my* prisoners."

This was said during a week when there was every prospect that General Grant would launch another attack as savage as that at the "Bloody Angle." Luckily for the Confederates, the heavy rains of the 11th and 12th continued long enough to soak the ground and to turn the dirt roads into streams of mud. By the time General Grant could move to another attack, Lee's men were rested and well able to meet their foe. A heavy assault on the 18th was beaten off with loss to the Federals. The next day an effort was made by Ewell to ascertain whether the Army of the Potomac was moving off. A brief, bloody action followed without material gain on either side. By the 21st of May, Grant was stirring. In that wooded country, either Army could slip away after darkness and steal a day's march on the other. Lee once more had to overtake his adversary or follow a shorter route—and always to keep between the Federals and Richmond.

CHAPTER SIXTEEN

The Battle Is Brought Back
to Richmond

BEHIND EWELL'S TROOPS, Lee left Spotsylvania on the night of May 21 and rode southward through the darkness. Two young soldiers from the countryside were his guides. After about fifteen miles of travel he came upon the rear of the Second Corps, from which numbers of soldiers had straggled. To all these tired, discouraged men Lee spoke in friendly exhortation, but from some of these who did not know him, he got tart answers. "Well you may order us to 'move on, move on'" one voice growled from the covering night, "when you are mounted on a horse and have all the rations that the country can afford!" Lee ignored this answer and was riding on when several of the stragglers came close enough to identify him. "Marse Robert!" they exclaimed. The other men got up on the instant and cheered him. "Yes, Marse Robert, we'll move on and go anywhere you say, even to hell."

The guides who witnessed this incident had occasion about day-light to see for themselves one of the qualities of Lee that aroused the devotion of his troops. When Lee halted for much-needed sleep, he asked the young men if they had any rations with them. Neither soldier had any food or much prospect of getting any, but both of them knew that the General could be little better off than they were as respects food, and they hesitated to reply. Lee guessed the reason for their vague answers. He told them to get feed for their horses from the nearest quartermaster and then to go to his headquarters tent for breakfast. Obediently the soldiers went, but all the General's orderly could find for them were two exceedingly bad biscuits each and a cup of some fluid that was grossly flattered to be called coffee. In this instance, Lee had not been able to do much in looking after his men but he had done all he could and he had treated his guides as individuals and as gentlemen, not as mere cogs in the war machine. They appreciated that.

The Confederate Army moved on to the North Anna River, crossed and took position there. Lee was sure that Grant would move in that direction and he was relieved that he got the Confederates to that high-banked little stream before the Federals reached there by the roundabout roads Grant had selected in order to march away secretly from Spotsylvania.

Precisely as had been anticipated, Union troops began to arrive on the farther bank of the North Anna about noon on the 23rd of May. Lee was still between them and Richmond, but he found them undeterred by his checkmate. Their artillery quickly opened against the Confederate bridgeheads; the Southern batteries replied. Lee happened at the moment to be on the lawn of Ellington, the Fox plantation, from which he observed the fire. At the insistence of the owner, Lee soon went from the lawn to the porch of the residence in order to drink a glass of buttermilk. While the General was there, a round shot from a Federal gun across the river passed within a few feet of him and imbedded itself in the doorframe. Lee continued to sip his milk and he did not move from his position till he had emptied the glass. Then he rode hastily away so that the enemy would not make the house a target.

Larger targets Grant had. The Federal commander had insisted from the opening of the campaign that a final Union victory was to be won by destroying Lee's troops, not by taking any city, even Richmond. Because the Confederate Army was his objective, Grant proceeded to attack on the North Anna. The ground was such that the Federals could cross the river on either flank of Lee, but they could not get a foothold on the south bank at the high point where the centre of the Southern line rested. The Confederate leader made the most of this. As a distinguished English military historian has put it, "Lee shut up his line like one closes an umbrella." Instead of a straight line on the river, the trenches of the gray Army became a capital "V." This offered the Confederates a great advantage, because Grant had to cross the river twice in shifting troops from one flank to the other.

Just at this favorable moment, when Lee was planning to strike at the Federals, he had a bad attack of diarrhoea. In the absence of the wounded Longstreet, there was nobody to whom Lee was willing to entrust the necessary moves. Lee kept saying "We must strike them a blow—we must never let them pass us again—we must strike them a blow," but it could not be done.

Grant did not know of Lee's illness, but he sensed his danger. On the night of May 26–27, Grant slipped away to escape the trap and then he moved down the North Anna in another effort to get between Lee and Richmond. The Confederates had to fall back closer to the capital in order to meet the new move by the left flank. This time, Lee's withdrawal brought him dangerously near Richmond and closer to an exciting situation that had existed ever since Grant had crossed the Rapidan on the 4th of May.

As a wily soldier, Grant had not relied solely on Meade's Army of the Potomac. That Army was the one with which Grant intended to destroy Lee, but three other small Armies had been set in motion when the main offensive began. The most troublesome of these lesser Armies —the only one that needs to be considered here—had been carried up James River from Fort Monroe on transports and had been landed on the right bank between Richmond and Petersburg, which is twenty-two miles south of Richmond. This so-called Army of the James was under Gen. B. F. Butler. It was to take Richmond, if possible, while Grant was overwhelming Lee. If Butler's Army could not do this, it was to occupy the attention of as many Confederate troops as it could engage.

To collect troops with whom to resist General Butler, the Confederate War Department had scoured the South Atlantic seaboard. All the men that could be moved on short notice were assembled around Petersburg and between that city and Richmond. Command of them was given Gen. P. G. T. Beauregard who, it will be remembered, had been one of the Confederate leaders in the First Battle of Manassas. In assailing this Confederate Army, Butler showed little military sense. He threw away excellent chances of taking Petersburg and of putting the greater part of the Richmond-Petersburg railroad behind his line. Then, after the Battle of Drewry's Bluff, on the 16th of May, he let himself be pushed back into Bermuda Neck, an area between the James and Appomattox Rivers. There, in Grant's own language, Butler was "bottled." The rivers were the wall of the bottle; the Confederate line was the cork.

After Butler was bottled, Lee suspected that Grant would send ships to Bermuda Neck and move part of the Army of the James to the Army of the Potomac, which already was receiving directly from the North many new troops to take the place of those who were killed or wounded or captured in the Wilderness and at Spotsylvania. If Butler's troops were added to Grant's, the odds against Lee would be heavier than ever—heavier, probably, than he could resist with success.

The only way to offset the expected new odds would be to bring some of Beauregard's troops to strengthen Lee. To this, at first, General Beauregard was much opposed. As Lee now drew closer to Richmond, he had to insist that his comrade across the river give him immediate help. Some of Butler's troops, Lee reasoned, certainly would join Grant in a few days. If the Army of Northern Virginia was not reinforced, Richmond might be lost.

While explaining all this, Lee moved swiftly back to cover the endangered city. Once again he correctly anticipated the direction of the Federal approach. When Grant crossed the Pamunkey River and approached Richmond from the northeast, the thin, unyielding gray line stood between the Union Army and the capital. Almost immediately there were indications that Grant was going to continue to move to the left. This would involve an extension of line. For that, Lee would not have sufficient men unless he received help from Beauregard.

While Lee was appealing desperately for aid, he thought he saw an opportunity of attacking part of the Federals on the 30th of May at Bethesda Church. The attack was made and was beaten off bloodily, but it added one fine memory to those the Army treasured. During the attack, young Col. Edward Willis of the famous Twelfth Georgia Regiment commanded the Brigade that suffered the heaviest losses. He was wounded frightfully and was aware that he could not recover. As his end approached swiftly, he uttered these fine words: "I am no more afraid to die than I was to go into the battle."

While Willis was breathing his last, after the futile Battle of Bethesda Church, a race for Cold Harbor was in progress. It proved to be among four entries—Lee's Army, Grant's host, heavy reenforcements from Butler to Grant and, finally, some help to Lee from Beauregard. The race scarcely could have been closer. The reenforcements arrived; the main Armies took position; the opposing forces looked at each other from behind earthworks that were being raised higher every hour.

The battle of the 1st of June was violent. On the 2nd, the forenoon was quiet, as if the enemy were planning some new blow. Most of the fighting of the afternoon was started by the Confederates, whose position near the Chickahominy Lee was trying to improve. A heavy rain that began prior to 4 o'clock was welcome reward for this effort, because the weather had been hot and dusty.

Soon after daylight on the 3rd of June, the rain having stopped, the Federals surged forward on the whole of their front. General Grant had lost patience. Like a desperate pugilist, he lowered his head, so to speak, and rushed at his adversary in a determination to slug it out then and there. At one point on Lee's right, the Federals reached the Southern trenches and held them for some time. On the centre, directly opposite the village of Cold Harbor, the blue line was repulsed so quickly and so completely that the assault was over before the gray-coats were fairly aroused to the fight. Elsewhere conditions varied with the ground and with the strength of the opposing troops but by 11 o'clock, the whole battle was over. Lee had watched the attack carefully though confidently. While the artillery was in full cry and 75,000 rifles were barking, a member of the cabinet and two Richmond lawyers of distinction came to headquarters on a tour of the front. "General," said one of them, as he listened to Grant's attack, "if he breaks your line, what reserve have you?"

Lee answered with his fullest candor: "Not a regiment—and that has been my condition ever since the fighting commenced on the Rappahannock. If I shorten my lines to provide a reserve, he will turn me; if I weaken my lines to provide a reserve, he will break them."

This was the daily plight of an Army now outnumbered almost two to one, but it was not yet so desperate a plight that Grant could afford to attack again as blindly as he did on the 3rd of June. He knew he had made a mistake in that assault and afterward he said so. At the time, he could not bring himself to ask for a truce during which he could get his wounded off the field and could bury the dead. Hour after hour, day after day, the Union soldiers who were perishing under the hot sun called out between the lines, "Water, water; for God's sake, water." Not until the 7th was a truce arranged. By that time, most of the Federal wounded had died. The battle meantime had lost its fury of combat and had become an ordeal of heat and stench and sharpshooting as sniping then was called.

Lee's lines held. Beauregard was in no immediate danger between Petersburg and Richmond. Those who did not know the true situation might have thought that Grant, like McClellan in 1862, had shot his bolt and would remain inactive in front of Richmond till driven or ordered away. Lee did not deceive himself. He knew that the Federals could replace all their losses and that he could not. It would not be possible, he told himself, to stand a long siege of Richmond with so small an army and with supplies and food pitifully limited.

In addition, Lee now found that he had to take part of his weakened forces and send them to Midland Virginia. Trouble was brewing there. At the time of Grant's advance from the Rapidan, a column of Federals had gone southward up the Shenandoah Valley, but had met with a defeat at New Market, where the cadets of V.M.I. had fought splendidly by the side of Confederate troops. After that action on May 15, the Federals had retreated but they now were sweeping forward again under a different commander, Maj. Gen. David Hunter. At Piedmont, June 6, Hunter defeated a Confederate force and took 1,000 prisoners. Then he pushed to Staunton, on the only railroad from the Shenandoah Valley to Richmond.

Hunter's advance was made at a time when almost all the Union cavalry under Gen. Philip Sheridan left the Army of the Potomac and started westward. It was thought by Lee that Sheridan might have been sent to help Hunter destroy property and to move eastward to join Grant. On the 11th and 12th of June, the Confederate cavalry met Sheridan at Trevilian Station, not far from Gordonsville, and forced him to retreat, but Hunter marched from Staunton to Lexington, the last town of any particular importance in the Upper Valley.

From Lexington, Hunter might move across the Blue Ridge Mountains and do much mischief. He must, therefore, be defeated and turned back. If that had to be undertaken, Lee reasoned that it should be done thoroughly by superior force, which afterward might proceed down the Valley and threaten Washington as "Stonewall" Jackson had in 1862. For this task, Lee chose the Second Corps, then under Lt. Gen. Jubal Early. To take from the army one of its three corps of infantry was to accept new risks of defeat, but those risks seemed preferable to standing by while Hunter tore up railroads and burned bridges and drove thousands of families from their homes.

On the day that General Early left Lee's Army for his long pursuit of Hunter, the scouts brought exciting news: The Federals had disappeared from Cold Harbor and from the whole line North and South of the village. Immediately the question was asked: Whither had Grant gone? He might retreat down the James River, but there was no known reason why he should. Perhaps he had moved toward James River in order to give himself elbow room for another blow at Lee. It was more probable that Grant was preparing to cross James River, so that he could cut off its supplies, a possibility of which the Confederate leaders frequently had talked. Whatever Grant's plan, it might not be disclosed for many hours. He had "stolen a march" again and had disappeared completely in a country of thick woods and few roads.

This was on the 13th of June. Two days later, General Beauregard reported that he was being attacked east of Petersburg. Beauregard had only 5,400 men to keep Butler corked in the bottle and to defend Petersburg. If the new attack on him was heavy, the troops might be some of those who had been sent from Butler to Grant and now were being returned to the south side of James River. There was an equal chance that the troops might be part of Grant's Army.

This uncertainty presented Lee one of the hardest problems of his life as a soldier. If he did not reenforce Beauregard at all, Petersburg and the nearby railroads might be lost; but if Lee sent too many of his troops to the Southside and later found that Grant still was on the Northside, then Lee might be too weak to keep Grant from capturing Richmond. Lee saw this clearly and he met the danger in this way: He kept urging General Beauregard to make prisoners of some of the Union troops in front of Petersburg and to find out whether they belonged to Butler's Army or to Grant's. At the same time, Lee began to send troops to Beauregard, a few thousand at a time. The remainder of the Army of Northern Virginia Lee held close to Richmond and to the bridges of boats across James River. This was done so that the men could move to Petersburg in a hurry or could defend Richmond if Grant attacked there.

While these things were being done on the 15th, 16th and 17th of June, Beauregard was having to demand of his little army all its courage and endurance. To hold Petersburg, he had to take away the few troops who formed the cork that bottled Butler. Immediately Butler's men poured out of their bottle and seized the railroad that joined Richmond and Petersburg.

This sacrifice did not give Beauregard nearly enough troops to hold back the Federals who continued to press him at Petersburg. On the evening of June 17 Lee received a telegram in which Beauregard said that he would have to abandon the earthworks he then was occupying. He would fall back toward a shorter line close to Petersburg. This new line, said Beauregard, he would hold as long as he could but if he did not get more help from Lee, he might have to give up Petersburg.

That was a dreadful prospect. For a few hours, it looked as if Lee would have to choose between Richmond and Petersburg. Almost at the very last moment, when a decision had to be made, Lee learned positively that the whole of Grant's Army was across the river. Instantly Lee dispatched orders for strong South Carolina troops to hurry to Petersburg to aid Beauregard. The next morning, June 18, when Beauregard's half-dead soldiers were moving into their new trenches, they looked toward the North from which help would come, and they saw in the light of the rising sun the glitter of the South Carolinians' bayonets. Richmond had been saved—and Petersburg, too!

CHAPTER SEVENTEEN

Petersburg Under Siege

THE ARRIVAL of Lee's Army in front of Petersburg on the 18th of June, 1864, was the beginning of what has always been called the "Siege of Petersburg." Actually, the word "siege" is not used accurately by soldiers except to describe what occurs when a city is cut off and surrounded so that it cannot get help or food from outside. That never happened at Petersburg until the very end of the war; but conditions were almost as bad in some ways as if the city had been under siege.

Lee now had to defend miles of trenches, which were close to those of the enemy and were subjected to a murderous fire of sharpshooters and mortars day and night. This was a new and hampering experience for Lee. He had won most of his victories by moving his troops fast and in unexpected directions. This sort of maneuver no longer was possible. The Army was held in its position by what was, so to speak, a short chain. Lee could not move far at any time without risking Richmond, or Petersburg or one of the railroads.

This condition was what soldiers call "loss of mobility." Along with it, there was a slow, steady loss of men. In the sun-baked, ill-smelling, fly-swarming trenches the soldiers often became sick. Those who died of disease or of wounds could not be replaced, because scarcely any recruits were reaching Lee. So many of the best officers had been killed in May and early June that the men might not have as good leadership as they had enjoyed before Gettysburg.

Everything else seemed to be declining. Rations were poorer, if possible, than they had been. Even when food was collected in the Far South and was put on freight-cars for the army, railroads broke down so often that provisions were slow in reaching the half-starved men at the front. All the while, the Confederates could see that Grant's Army remained strong and was becoming more confident of its power and of the excellence of its leadership. Food and medical care were abundant on the other side. Troops and strong horses always were available for anything Grant wanted to undertake. Lee, in contrast, had to search for the men to do even the necessary things. The horses of his Army were fewer and feebler. For the first time, some of the stout-hearted soldiers were beginning to doubt whether the Confederacy could survive against such odds.

General Lee knew better than anyone else, except the President, how adverse those odds were, but he never intimated to anyone that he believed the Southern cause was becoming hopeless. He probably shut his well-disciplined mind to all thought of defeat. Besides, Lee found a certain reassurance in being able, time after time, to meet and to beat the invaders in small actions undertaken to protect the railroads. Less than a week after Lee established headquarters at Petersburg, the Federals under Gen. James H. Wilson tried to tear up two railways that connected Petersburg with Southside Virginia and with Western North Carolina. Wilson was stopped at Staunton River by a small force of soldiers and citizens under a daring young Confederate captain named L. B. Farinholt. Then Wilson was chased back to Grant's Army by the Confederate cavalry. They said he "tore up" the railroads and then "tore down" the dirt roads in order to escape pursuit. Lee was not deceived by Wilson's hurried return. The breaks on the railroads would be hard to repair and were a warning of what had to be expected elsewhere.

While the fate of the railroads still was uncertain, army engineers brought Lee reports of a danger he never had faced before. It was certain, the engineers said, that Federals were digging underground at a point near Petersburg where the Union and Confederate lines were close together. The sound of picks could be heard plainly. Soon afterward, in mirrors hung high in trees near the front, the Federals could be seen hauling out dirt from beneath a hill. The Southern soldiers at first made fun of this. When veterans went into Petersburg with a new recruit, they would tell him that Grant already had carried his tunnel as far as the main business street of the town, and that the Federals were using a locomotive and cars in the tunnel. The recruit was assured that if he put his ear to the ground and listened intently, he could hear the sound of the train. If he looked with care, they said, he could see the smoke from the locomotive rising from among the cobblestones.

This was a good gag but soon the men began to get anxious. It was not pleasant to spend all day in those oven-like trenches and then to lie down at night with the reflection that one might be awakened by being blown sky high in the middle of the night. Some ingenious soldiers developed a boring device by which they could at least make certain that no Federal mine was close to the surface under their part of the line. Lee went further than this. He had the engineers dig tunnels of their own in the hope that they would strike those the enemy were preparing. Often, deep in the earth, the Confederates could hear every blow the blue workers struck, but the Southern miners never had the good fortune to encounter the Unionists.

Just before daylight on the 30th of July, a deep roar and a wide tremor of the earth told the Confederates that the mine had been exploded. Tons of red earth, lifted by 8,000 pounds of powder, had buried at least 278 South Carolina troops and had torn a great hole thirty feet deep, 135 feet along the trenches and approximately ninety-five feet from front to rear. Into the crater of the mine, the Federals at once rushed many troops, white and colored. These men should have spread out immediately up and down the trenches and should have tried to break through while the Confederates still were dazed by the shock. Instead of doing this, the Federals themselves were half-bewildered. Most of them climbed down into the crater and stayed there. A few hundred brave men in blue undertook to seize the lines but they failed.

In a short while, Confederate artillery was pouring shells into the crater and into those parts of the trenches occupied by the enemy. General Lee soon rode up from his quarters across the river and placed troops where he hoped they could hold the ground behind the crater until a charge could be made to recapture the line. About the time the Confederates were ready to deliver this charge, some of the Federals attempted to move downhill so as to deepen the breach, but this advance merely gave the Confederates a new target.

At length the Southerners undertook to recover the lost ground. Virginians, Georgians, North Carolinians and Alabamians dashed up the hill. With them went the few South Carolina troops who had survived the explosion. Hard fighting was demanded of all these men. Several attacks had to be made before the lines were restored and the Federals were killed or captured or were forced to run the gauntlet back to their lines. When the Confederates at last could look down into the crater, it was a cauldron of dead and dying. Soldiers got some idea of the force of the explosion by observing that a great mass of clay as large as a cabin had mounted high in the air and had fallen to the ground intact.

One Confederate soldier, with a glorious sense of humor, professed a greater marvel. During the fight to recapture the crater he came up to an officer. He had been blown up in the explosion, he explained, and wanted to get even. Might he go into the charge with the Alabama troops?

"Yes," said the officer, "who are you?"

The soldier gave his name and the number of his South Carolina regiment and asked the officer to write them down so that, if he were killed, his own commanders might be notified.

He was told that time did not permit any writing. "How high were you blown?" the officer asked.

"I don't know," said the South Carolinian, "but as I was going up I met the company commissary officer coming down, and he said, 'I will try to have breakfast ready by the time you get down.'"

The spirit of most of the men who participated in the Battle of the Crater was equally fine. As that victory came not long after certain encouraging events that will be described in the next chapter, Confederate prospects brightened for a time but for a short time only. Then Lee found that the army had another difficulty to overcome: The Federal commander had so many troops that without weakening his line, he could move thousands of men easily from one side of James River to the other. While pretending to attack around Petersburg, Grant could assail Richmond, or vice versa. There was only one way, so far as Lee could discover, of dealing with this shifting of force. That was to thin his line still further and to keep some good troops opposite Bermuda Neck, from which they could be hurried quickly either to Richmond or to Petersburg.

While Lee was on the north side of the river, dealing with one of these threats against Richmond, he had another interesting experience with one of a group of Federals who had been captured after a pursuit. The bluecoat came boldly up to Lee and explained that a Confederate had taken his hat. That was in a day when most Americans thought it dangerous for a man to go bareheaded. Loss of a hat was a serious matter. Lee listened and then told the Federal to point out the man who had snatched his hat. The soldier did so. Lee went over, made the Confederate return the head covering and then went on with the orders he had been giving when interrupted. The circumstance was a small one but it made its impression. Said one of the Unionists: "I wondered at him taking any notice of a prisoner in the midst of battle. It showed what a heart he had for them."

Before Lee could return to his headquarters after this fight on the Northside, Grant attacked on the Southside and pushed forward to the Petersburg and Weldon Railroad. General Beauregard immediately undertook to recover the railway but he could not do so. Although a successful attack was made by some of Lee's men against Federals at Reams Station, August 24, the Federals' grip on the track could not be shaken. Lee had to abandon the use of the northern end of the railway. All supplies that came to the army by that route had to be hauled by wagon over twenty miles of sandy roads.

Little enough of food for the army and even less, relatively, of corn and oats came for the animals. Men and horses were on short rations. That was why on September 16, the army rejoiced over an exploit by Gen. Wade Hampton, who had succeeded to command of Stuart's cavalry. Through George Shadburne, one of the most cunning scouts, Hampton learned that about 3,000 beef cattle belonging to the Federal Army were near Coggin's Point on the south side of the James River. With Lee's approval, Hampton decided to make an effort to get these beeves. He took a strong force of his mounted men, rode a long way around the Union outposts, attacked the enemy near Sycamore Church, herded 2,486 of the cattle, and got all except eighteen of these to the Confederate lines. For days after that the soldiers had beef instead of the thin slice of "Nassau bacon" that had been issued them. The temporary contrast between fat beef and rancid bacon gave point to a joke that then was going the rounds of the educated soldiers. They of course were proud to call themselves the Army of Northern Virginia, but for a shorter name they preferred now to be known as "Lee's Army." Still another name, they said in grim jest, was appropriate to them. Victor Hugo's novel *Les Misérables* was being republished in the South and was much read in the army. The title seemed distinctly personal to the men: They were Lee's Miserables, they said.

CHAPTER EIGHTEEN

In the Face of Defeat

G ENERAL LEE's constant appeals for his "Miserables" was that they get better rations, good clothing and shoes, and that the gaps in their ranks be filled by men who had dodged the conscription act. In 1861 Lee had been proud of the volunteers who made up as large an army as the Confederacy then could equip; but before the spring of 1862, Lee had seen that the only way of opposing successfully the great strength of the more populous Northern States was to put in the Confederate Army every man capable of carrying a rifle. All able-bodied men, Lee believed, should fight in defence of rights that were enjoyed by all. Nothing made him so angry as the knowledge that while his soldiers were starving and marching and dying, other men of like age and physical fitness were doing nothing for the Southern cause. Steadily in the autumn of 1864 his warning to the government became more and more serious. He told the President: ". . . We have no troops disposable to meet movements of the enemy or strike when opportunity presents, without taking them from the trenches and exposing some important point. The enemy's position enables him to move his troops to the right or left without our knowledge, until he has reached the point at which he aims, and we are then compelled to hurry our men to meet him, incurring the risk of being too late to check his progress and the additional risk of the advantage he may derive from their absence."

It was this more frequent shifting of the attack from the north side of the James to the south, and from the south side of the river to the north that tested Lee and his Army to the fullest during weeks when every chill wind brought bad news from other parts of the Confederacy. Jubal Early's campaign against the Federals who had marched up the Valley was most successful at first. Attacked at Lynchburg, General Hunter retreated into Western Virginia, and then fled where no man pursued. Thereupon, Early moved down the Shenandoah Valley, advanced unopposed into Maryland, defeated a Federal Army on the Monocacy River, July 9, and headed straight for Washington. His advance created tense alarm. Many of his own men and most of his opponents thought he intended to attack the city, but the task was too much for his small force of less than 13,000 men. Early realized this after looking at the Federal fortifications on the morning of July 12. He knew, also, that reinforcements for Washington had arrived from Grant's Army.

Regretfully, then, Early had to retreat to Virginia but he raised Southern hopes which the Battle of the Crater temporarily strengthened. For two months, Early held off a steadily-enlarged Federal Army under command of Maj. Gen. Phil Sheridan. About the middle of September, Lee had to recall some of the troops he had sent to Early after the Battle of the Monocacy. As soon as Sheridan learned that these troops were leaving the Valley, he attacked and defeated Early near Winchester. This was on the 19th of September. Three days later, September 22, Sheridan struck again at Fisher's Hill and compelled Early to retreat toward Staunton.

This was grim news for Lee to add to many reports of lost battles and lost positions of value in the Far South. The bad tidings from Early came, also, at the time of one of the most dangerous shifts from the South to the North of the James that Grant ever made. About seven miles below Richmond, the river runs under some bluffs and then turns sharply East before it resumes its southerly course. The Confederates in 1862 had taken advantage of this bend in the river to construct heavy forts at each end of the East-and-West stretch. If warships entered that part of the river, they could be attacked from front and rear. The earthworks on the south side of the river were at Drewry's Bluff. Those on the North bank were at Chafin's Bluff. The rear of Chafin's Bluff was on high, level ground. To protect the fortification on the bluff that guarded the river, long lines of trenches had been built. Among these were several forts, the largest of which was called Fort Harrison.

On the 29th of September, General Lee received a dispatch in which General Ewell announced that Fort Harrison had been captured by a surprise attack that morning. This exposed the whole of the Richmond defences as well as the approaches of Chafin's Bluff. If possible, the breach in the defences of the capital city had to be repaired. Lee stripped temporarily the works around Petersburg and hurried troops across the river to recover the lost fort. That afternoon late, as the General was riding alone behind the lines he came upon a very young and small soldier who was carrying many canteens. Lee, of course, was intensely concerned over the fort, but he had built up by daily self-control so complete a mastery of himself that he could be calm and considerate of others even when his own nerves were strained. "What are you doing behind, my little fellow?" he asked in his kindly, grave tone.

The boy explained that he had stopped at a well to fill the canteens of some of the men of his company.

"Well," said Lee, "hurry and catch up; they will need you by daylight." Doubtless the suggestion that he would be needed for winning a victory inspired the young soldier. He started at a trot to over-take his command, and when he arrived he had a tall tale to relate of what "Marse Robert" had told him would happen the next day.

It did not happen as Lee had hoped. The soldiers who made the first attack to regain Fort Harrison could not strike together at the proper time. When they failed to reach the Federal line, Lee rode out to the North Carolina troops, who were among the best in the entire army. In words that were few but earnest, he appealed to them to make another effort. They did so, with much gallantry, but for a second time they failed. Lee still believed the fort could be retaken. One fighter who happened to be near at hand wrote later: "I had al-ways thought General Lee was a very cold and unemotional man, but he showed lots of feeling and excitement on this occasion; even the staid and stately Traveller caught the spirit of his master, and was prancing and cavorting while the General was imploring his men to make one more effort to take the position for him." North Carolina troops seldom turned back when they undertook anything. They re-sponded to the plea of "Marse Robert" and threw themselves for a third time against the earthworks. It was too strong for them.

The repulse of the final attack of September 30 convinced General Lee that he must find a new way of taking the fort. He studied the situation for almost a week and then decided that he might keep the Federals in Fort Harrison from doing further harm if he could seize the trenches the bluecoats had captured North of the great mounds of earth that had defied attack from the front. Carefully Lee worked out a plan which he explained to the Generals who were to direct the fighting on the 7th of October. They understood what he wanted them to do, but when the attack was delivered, the troops somehow could not strike in the one-two-three manner that Lee ordered. In the midst of the fighting one young soldier of 18 or 19 came up to Lee and said, "General, if you don't send more men down there, our boys will get hurt sure!"

Lee turned to him and saw that the soldier's uniform was bloody: "Are you wounded, my boy?" Lee inquired.

"Yes, sir."

"Where are you wounded?"

"I'm shot through both arms, General, but I don't mind that, General. I want you to send some more men down there to help our boys."

Even that fine spirit could not win the fight against the heavy odds. The Florida Brigade wore itself out in a gallant attack. Several other units did equally well, but they could not break the Federal grip on Fort Harrison. Lee had to leave the fort in the hands of the enemy while he had the men build a new line in front of it to protect Chafin's Bluff from a surprise attack.

About two weeks later Lee had assurance that the Northside would be watched with vigilance and defended with stubborn skill. The bullet that struck Longstreet in the Wilderness on May 6 had torn the right shoulder and had almost paralyzed the arm, but it had not shaken the nerve of the General. He had gone to a quiet town where he had good nursing, and when he found that he could not use his right hand, he taught himself to write with the left. Now, after a little more than five months, he was back in place, still crippled in his arm but able to direct his famous First Corps. Lee gladly and confidently turned over to Longstreet the protection of the Northside which from that time, October 19, was as safe as Lee could expect it to be while defended by so few men against so many.

In the whole of the unequal fight between the North and the South, Lee never had been able to make the most of any victory or to use to the fullest for any length of time the service of his most capable lieutenants. Always something happened to mar a success or to tie the hands of an able man. It was so, once again, after Longstreet's return to duty. The very day that Longstreet relieved Lee's mind of concern over the Northside, General Early sustained another and a still worse defeat at Cedar Creek in the Shenandoah Valley.

This was one of the strangest battles of the entire war. General Early had advanced down the Valley again as soon as he had received troops to take the place of those lost at Winchester and at Fisher's Hill in September. On the 19th of October, Early caught the Federals off guard and drove them back from Cedar Creek to the vicinity of Middletown. There he halted his men in the belief that the beaten Federals would continue to withdraw. Instead, the Union commander, General Sheridan, hurried from Winchester, renewed the fight and forced Early to retreat.

This Battle of Cedar Creek lost to the Confederates nearly all the Shenandoah Valley. Lee was not blamed for the defeat but Early was condemned and denounced. He did not deserve some of the criticism heaped on him. The odds against him had been greater than he could overcome, though he had accepted those odds courageously. He knew that he was fighting at a disadvantage, but he was holding many thousand troops who otherwise would have been used against Lee and against the Confederate capital. This fine spirit was cancelled, unfortunately, by some military vices. Early's chief fault in this campaign was that he had a prejudice against some of the cavalry under his command. He did not know much about using cavalry and, because of his prejudice, he would not learn.

Loss of the Shenandoah Valley meant the loss of the food it would have supplied the half-starved army. Equally serious was the fact that Lee no longer had any way of threatening Washington. So long as he could move troops down the Shenandoah, he always had a good chance of forcing Grant to send part of the Army of the Potomac to defend the Federal capital. President Lincoln had become very nervous about the safety of the city after the Valley Campaign of 1862. Lee had made the most of Lincoln's fears and had hoped when he sent Early to the Shenandoah that he could relieve some of the pressure on Richmond. If Grant reduced the size of the Federal Army by sending troops to protect Washington, then Lee could hope to attack Grant when the odds were not too heavy.

That hope was gone now. Lee had to fight it out with Grant while held to the Richmond-Petersburg defences by a shortened chain. After the war, many persons were curious to know when General Lee saw that final defeat could not be avoided. Nobody dared ask General Lee that question, but his staff officers received many inquiries. It was the opinion of some of the members of General Lee's staff that he saw after Early's defeat in the Valley that the Confederate cause was doomed. If this were true, it did not dispose Lee to think that he should quit the fight. So long as the President and the Congress believed the war should be continued, he would obey orders. Once during the winter of 1864–65, when the dark outlook had become black, Lee was talking with Colonel Venable about the difficulty of defending his long line with so few troops. Venable asked why Lee did not abandon the line. Lee turned on him instantly and said, in effect, "To do that would be to be a traitor to the government."

CHAPTER NINETEEN

A Black Christmas for Lee's Army

AFTER EARLY'S DEFEAT at Cedar Creek, every task of Lee was harder to perform. As autumn turned to winter, the fortunes of the Confederacy seemed to fall with the season. In the Far South, General W. T. Sherman was marching through Georgia to the sea. Lee's faithful lieutenant, John B. Hood, had turned away from fighting Sherman and had moved into Tennessee where defeat soon overwhelmed him. In Lee's own army, cowards began to creep away in the darkness and left their comrades to fight against still heavier odds. Even some of the faithful men who had stuck to their colors through the entire war lost heart. The army slowly grew weaker and weaker because of desertion. Rations were smaller than ever and of even poorer quality. The "Nassau bacon" issued the soldiers was so bad that the men jokingly said the Federals let it pass through the blockade of Southern ports in order to poison the Confederate Army. Wood for camp fires grew scarcer. Thin and ragged uniforms could not always be replaced. To keep themselves from freezing when they were not stirring, the men in the trenches had to make themselves dug-outs. Officially these were called "bomb-proofs," but in the conversation of the men they were known as "rat-holes."

Every possible way of driving Grant's strong, well-fed and warmly-clad Army from in front of Richmond and of Petersburg was studied by Lee, but nothing could be done to keep the Union forces from pressing hard and harder. Grant had men enough to continue steadily the lengthening of the line. Every time Lee extended his line to match Grant's, he increased the danger of the parts from which he took troops. On a vast scale, the situation was much as if one man were opening with both hands a thick, strong rubber band while the man opposite him had a thin, weak band, which he had to stretch equally far. It was as certain as anything could be that the feebler band would be stretched to the breaking-point. The pulling of the "rubber band" was always to the westward, because Grant knew that the Confederates depended largely on the Southside Railroad (now the Norfolk and Western). When Grant's left was extended far enough to reach that railroad, Lee no longer would be able to supply his Army. Many who understood this wondered why Lee did not leave Petersburg and Richmond and carry the war to the interior. During the autumn, this was not done because the Confederate government still believed it could win. After winter came, the roads were so muddy that Lee knew his feeble, underfed horses could not pull the wagons or the guns. The Confederate Army had to stay where it was and beat off the Federals until the bottomless roads dried in the warm sun of spring. Even when spring came in 1865, other conditions might be worse, rather than better. Sherman might march up the South Atlantic coast through the Carolinas to reinforce Grant.

In this daily struggle with calamity, Lee and his lieutenants labored to stop desertion, to reduce the terrible hardships of the trenches, and to keep the men cheerful and in good fighting spirit. Lee set the example. He had little at his table that the soldier in the "rat-hole" did not have. Once when General Ewell came to consult him at Petersburg, Lee could not provide any food for the guest except by insisting that Ewell eat his lunch. It consisted of two cold sweet potatoes. An Irish member of the British Parliament, visiting Lee's headquarters,

GENERAL ROBERT E. LEE
TOWARD THE END OF THE WAR

Photo by Vannerson of Richmond. Courtesy, Valentine Museum, Richmond

told a friend that Lee had only two biscuits for lunch that day and gave him one of them. Another day the visitor went back to Petersburg with an enthusiastic report: "What a glorious dinner today, madam! Somebody sent 'Uncle Robert' a box of sardines."

As Christmas approached, the women of Richmond determined that they would give the soldiers in the trenches at least one good meal during the holidays. Appeals for food were sent merchants and farmers. Before anyone could determine whether the response would be adequate, word spread among the camps that a feast would be prepared. A member of the Eighteenth Georgia thus described what happened: ". . . our mouths 'watered' till January 1, 1865. On that day all who were able to do so got up very early. The army was to do nothing. The ladies were to do all. They would provide all vehicles, and the 'goodies' would be taken right along the lines and distributed to the half-famished men by dainty hands. And we waited. What a long day that seemed to be! We whiled away the tedious hours by telling stories and cracking jokes! Noon came, then two, four, eight, ten, and twelve o'clock, and still no 'goody' wagon. Being still a little weak, I became tired and lay down and went to sleep with the understanding that those on watch would call me when our dinner arrived. It was after 3 A.M. when a comrade called and told me that a detail had just gone out to meet the precious wagon and bring in our feast. But oh what a disappointment when the squad returned and issued to each man only one small sandwich made up of two tiny slices of bread and a thin piece of ham! A few men ventured to inquire, 'Is this all?' But I think they were ashamed of themselves the next moment. After the 'meal' was finished a middle-aged corporal lighted his pipe and said: 'God bless our noble women! It was all they could do; it was all they had.' And then every man in that old tent indulged in a good cry. We couldn't help it." The corporal had stated the truth. Within the region from which food could be sent quickly to the committee of ladies, there was nothing "good" to send.

At General Lee's headquarters, conditions at Christmas were a little different but to his staff officers were equally disappointing. The General himself was invited to dine in Petersburg with a family that had contrived to get a turkey. Lee would have relished eating part of the fowl because he had an excellent appetite and enjoyed good food, but he did not touch the serving of white meat and dark that was put on his plate. His hostess noticed this and mustered up her courage to ask if the General did not care for turkey. Lee doubtless reddened at the embarrassing question and then admitted, in some confusion, that he was saving his portion in the hope he could take it with him and give it to one of his staff officers who was sick and had "nothing to eat but corn bread and sweet-potato coffee." The hostess of course saw to it that some turkey was put aside for the staff officer so that the General could eat his.

Other admirers sent from a distance a barrel full of turkeys to the General's headquarters. In his absence one of the staff officers opened the barrel and spread out all the turkeys. The largest was to be for the General. All the others were picked in turn by the different members of the staff as their own. Many plans were made for arranging turkey dinners to which the friends of individual officers would be invited. Unfortunately for them, when the General came in and saw the turkeys, he directed immediately that the one set aside for him should be sent to the nearest hospital. He said this in such a tone that his staff knew he wanted them to do the same thing. Sorrowfully they repacked the fowls in the barrel, which was carried to the quarters of sick soldiers nearby.

For the men who could go to Richmond or to Petersburg on brief leave of absence, Lee encouraged such social affairs as the two courageous cities could provide. Almost all entertainment was without refreshment, because none could be provided, but even these "starvation parties" were considered of doubtful patriotism. Many persons said there should be no festivity and, in particular, no dances when the Southern cause was desperate. After much argument among themselves concerning the dances, some of the young Richmond hostesses agreed that they would leave the question to General Lee. When he was told by one of the girls that they had pledged themselves not to dance a step if he disapproved, he answered at once: "Why of course, my dear child! My boys need to be heartened up when they get furloughs. Go on, look your prettiest, and be just as nice to them as ever you can be!"

The General himself did not have time to attend parties. He could not even go often to Richmond where Mrs. Lee, her daughters and her friends spent most of their time knitting for soldiers. Pair after pair of woolen socks were distributed by the General where they were most needed. To get his mind off the miseries of war for a few hours, Lee occasionally would send into Petersburg and have nurses bring out to his headquarters at Edge Hill a few little girls to play where he could watch them. This gave the children some relief from the sound and danger of the frequent bombardment of Petersburg at the same time that their presence comforted him. Once, at least, a visit of this sort was marred. The General was riding back to the city in a wagon with some of his little guests when one of them "showed off" by striking the mules with the whip in order to make them go faster. Lee mildly rebuked her, but she repeated the performance. "Anne," he said, "you must not do that again. My conscience is not entirely at ease about using these animals for this extra service, for they are half fed, as we all are."

Other visitors he found pleasant or vexing, as the case might be, but he made it his rule to see, if possible, all those who called on him. A reward for this democratic hospitality came from the humblest of his visitors, a Negro cook.

"General Lee," said the man, "I been wantin' to see you a long time. I's a soldier."

"Ah—to which army do you belong, to the Union army or to the Southern army?"

"Oh, General," the man answered proudly, "I b'long to your army."

"Well, have you been shot?"

The visitor was a little puzzled: "Naw, sah, I ain' been shot yet."

"How is that? Nearly all our men get shot."

"Why, General, I ain' been shot 'case I stays back whar de generals stay."

That brought a smile to the face of Lee at a time when smiles were few. A dark cause was becoming desperate. From the South the worst of news poured in. Sherman was marching northward to join Grant. Wilmington, N. C., the last port through which the Confederates were getting supplies from Europe, was captured by the Federals. The railroads were breaking down. Desertion was worse than ever. On the 6th of February Lee was made General-in-chief of all the Confederate Armies, but he was unable to direct the small, scattered forces which the Federals were steadily pressing into a smaller and small part of Virginia and North Carolina. Efforts to make peace failed. Hopeless as the outlook appeared, most Southerners still believed that Lee and his Army once again would defeat the Federals and would win Southern independence. A little earlier in the year, General Lee had told Mrs. Lee "I pray daily and almost hourly to our Heavenly Father to come to the relief of you and our afflicted country. I know He will order all things for our good, and we must be content." To the Secretary of War he wrote in March: "Everything, in my opinion, has depended and still depends upon the dispositions and feelings of the people." Unless those at home were willing to give more, they would lose all.

CHAPTER TWENTY

A Week-long Nightmare for Lee

ON THE NIGHT of April 1, 1865, when Lee lay down to take a few hours' rest at Edge Hill, the Federal artillery was roaring defiantly along the whole line. For almost four years, Lee had faced that artillery and the great army behind it, but never had he been in so desperate a plight as he was that night. On the 25th of March, he had made at Fort Stedman an effort to break through the Federal trenches, but he had failed with heavy loss. Now he had news that Sheridan with the Union cavalry from the Shenandoah Valley had rejoined Grant and had started a powerful movement to get around the Confederate right and to cut the Southside Railroad. Lee did not have sufficient cavalry to meet the stronger mounted bluecoats. He had been compelled to use infantry to help his small cavalry columns. It was a clumsy, almost hopeless arrangement. Before retiring that evening Lee had received vague reports that this mixed Confederate force had been defeated at a place known as Five Forks. Details were few but disaster was in the air.

Before daylight on the 2nd of April, General A. P. Hill arrived at Lee's Headquarters. He had heard an unverified rumor of a break somewhere on the long Confederate line. No definite information had been sent him. The only unusual condition was the vigor of the artillery fire. This was furious for so early an hour. The rifles of the pickets were rattling. All along the front the enemy was astir. Soon after Hill arrived, Longstreet came also. He had been summoned from the Northside with part of his small Corps in order that he might help repair the damage done at Five Forks.

While Lee was explaining where he wished Longstreet's troops to be placed, a staff officer broke into the room with amazing news: Past the headquarters, teamsters were lashing their mules and were hurrying their wagons toward Petersburg. These men said that the Federals had overrun the Confederate trenches and were driving out the Confederates. The officers in Lee's room sprang up. Longstreet hurried off to his troops. A. P. Hill quickly took horse and hastened forward, because the break was on his part of the thin and weary line. Lee dressed, mounted and rode out in front of Headquarters.

Soon he ascertained that the dreadful report of a break was true. General Hill already had been met by Federals and had been killed. Almost the whole of the right of the Confederate line had been swept away. The only troops on whom Lee now could depend for the defence of Petersburg were those who remained in the trenches to the left.

If these were all the men who stood in front of the enemy, Petersburg could not be held beyond that fatal day. When Petersburg was abandoned, Richmond had to be. Whether or not the roads were firm enough for the teams to pull the wagons and the guns through the mud, a retreat had to be made. It must be directed toward the Roanoke River and toward Johnston's army in North Carolina.

Swiftly and grimly Lee gave the necessary first orders. The young officer who was closest to him that day wrote afterward: "Self-contained and serene, he acted as one who was conscious of having accomplished all that was possible in the line of duty, and who was undisturbed by the adverse conditions in which he found himself. There was no apparent excitement and no sign of apprehension as he issued his orders for the retreat of his sadly reduced army and the relinquishment of the position so long and successfully held against the greatly superior force opposed to him . . . It was a striking illustration of Christian fortitude, the result of an habitual endeavor to faithfully perform the duties of one's station, and of unquestioning trust in the decrees of an all-wise Creator. . . ."

Once only did Lee personally show the fighting spirit that shaped every order even in this moment of disaster. Edge Hill had to be abandoned. It was in the line of Federal advance and soon was aflame. From the house Lee rode a little way toward the city, to open new headquarters, and for some minutes he was under artillery fire. A shell broke near him and scattered fragments. Lee's face flushed. With a tight rein on Traveller he turned in his saddle and looked back at the Federals as if he were resolved to wheel about and, with his staff-officers, to charge them. After an inward struggle he speedily recovered his grip on himself and proceeded to a residence about a mile from Petersburg. From that house, over a hastily-strung telegraph wire, detailed orders now were sent for the withdrawal that night of the troops around Richmond and those between the capital and Petersburg. The direction of the retreat was explained in telegrams prepared for the officers who were responsible for moving food and supplies.

That fateful night, Petersburg was abandoned by all the troops who had defended the line from the Appomattox River to the point where the enemy had broken through and had cut off the right wing. The thin Confederate Brigades were withdrawn from the red trenches after dark. Nearly all the artillery was removed, also. Lee himself rode on Traveller and had little to say, but afterward he confessed that his heart was wrung at the thought of leaving the women and children of Petersburg to the mercy of the Federals.

So quietly did the Confederates leave that the enemy was unaware till morning of the beginning of the retreat. Lee had stolen a march just as Grant had at Spotsylvania and at Cold Harbor.

If Lee had good luck and met with no delay, he should be able to keep ahead. His route was the best that could have been chosen to bring together quickly all the Confederate troops on a railroad from which they could get supplies. The column from Petersburg was to move West until it reached the Richmond and Danville Railroad at Amelia Court House, which is about thirty-five miles from the starting-point. By the time the troops from Petersburg got to Amelia, those from Richmond and its vicinity were expected to join them. All of them then would move down the railroad in the direction of Danville. Somewhere South of that city, Johnston with his little Army would be awaiting Lee.

Everything went well on April 3, the first day out of Petersburg. When Lee stopped, on invitation, for dinner at Clover Hill, the Cox plantation, young Kate Cox said to him reassuringly: "We shall still gain our cause; you will join General Johnston and together you will be victorious."

"Whatever happens," Lee answered, "know this—that no men ever fought better than those who have stood by me."

As he passed his soldiers on the road that day, he found them cheerful and not exhausted by their march. They were hungry, of course, because most of them had eaten all the scant ration issued before they left Petersburg, but that was not a serious concern. The men were accustomed to being hungry. Besides, they would reach Amelia and their train of provisions the next morning. So thought Lee; so believed all the officers and all the men who knew the course of the roads and of the railway.

Then, on the 4th, fate intervened. When the leading troops arrived at the quiet little village, no supply-train was at the station. The railroad agent had no report of any cars on the way to Amelia. No rations were in storage there. The residents scarcely had enough food for themselves.

Lee was aghast. His army was in the most critical retreat of the war and was without even cornbread and bacon! The only possible way of getting anything to eat immediately was to stop the Army, to send wagons out into the district around the Court House, and to borrow or beg or buy from the farmers. While waiting for the wagon, the Army would lose the march that had been gained on the night of the 2nd. The enemy might catch up! As quickly as possible, Lee telegraphed for rations to be sent from Danville. An appeal to the farmers was printed and distributed; wagons were sent out; the men waited hungrily and wondered why provisions had not been sent. Lee could not answer. He did not know then and he never learned in his lifetime why trains were not loaded in Richmond and moved to Amelia. Even now the reason is not plain. The most probable explanation is that the orders were not sent from Petersburg until so late that when they reached Richmond, the city was in mad confusion. Nobody was left to find or to load cars.

During the night of the 4th–5th and on the morning of the 5th, the army wagons returned from the district around Amelia. Every heart sank at the sight of them. Scarcely anything had been collected. The farms had been stripped already, or else corn and flour and meat had been hidden so skillfully that the men on the wagons could not find them.

This was not the only bad news. Just as had been expected, the enemy was catching up. Some of his cavalry had been hovering South of Amelia during the afternoon of the 4th. More of them could be expected on the 5th. No courageous man liked to think of such a thing, but the Federal infantry might overtake the Confederates and

Photo by W. Gordon Hill

RICHMOND IN FLAMES

LITHOGRAPH BY CURRIER & IVES IN THE VIRGINIA STATE LIBRARY

get across the line of retreat down the Richmond and Danville Railroad.

No more time could be lost. That was certain. If the Army waited around Amelia, the Federals would cut the railroad by which provisions could be brought from Danville. Then hunger would become starvation. Weakened as the soldiers were by their long fast, Lee had to order them to start down the railroad in the hope that they could keep ahead of the bluecoats and could meet the trains that would be sent from Danville. It was a cruel order: not to have given it would have been still more cruel. By 1 P.M. on the 5th, Longstreet's troops began to move by a road that almost paralleled the railway. Most of the other infantry prepared to follow. Those from Richmond had arrived at Amelia or were approaching, and would pursue the same route.

Wearily under gray and sobbing skies, the old First Corps plodded onward. At a distance of about seven miles from Amelia, beyond the village of Jetersville, the infantry were halted. Cavalrymen who were covering the advance had sent back word of suspicious movements on a low ridge that ran across the railroad a short distance southwest of Jetersville. As soon as Lee heard this, he rode forward and began to study the ground. A heart less stout than his would have failed: Federals in considerable number—infantry, cavalry or both— were in the stretch of forest on the ridge. They had built trenches, too. These were visible, but Lee could not see enough of the ground to ascertain whether his men could get around the Federal trenches and resume the march. He sent for farmers who lived in the neighborhood and questioned them on the direction of the roads and the course of the streams. Soon he saw that the natives knew little that the maps did not show.

Lee consequently had to decide for himself the fateful question of attacking or skirting the ridge. Slowly and carefully, almost yard by yard, he examined the ground with his glasses. If he went on, he could follow the shortest route to North Carolina, though an assault would mean death to many soldiers in an army that already was too small to meet the Federals in the open. There was a difficult and dangerous alternative. Instead of making an attack or slipping around the flank of the enemy, Lee could leave the Richmond and Danville Railroad and strike across country to the westward. If the Army could hold together for a march of fifteen or twenty miles, it could reach the upper part of the Southside Railroad. Down that track, supplies could be sent from Lynchburg. After the Army had been rationed, it could swing southward again to unite with Johnston.

Which should it be, a battle or a march to the other railway? Lee's reconnaissance would decide that. At last, he finished his examination of the ground. He put down his glasses and shook his head. The position was strong, an assault might prove too costly. Hard as was the alternative, it must be accepted: The army must wait till darkness and then it must try to reach the Southside Railroad near the town of Farmville.

That night march should have been called a nightmare. Some of the men who had eaten their last rations at midday April 3 had now been almost sixty hours without food. The feebler of the soldiers began to drop by the roadside. Some wandered off in search of food and never got back to the column. Brave men, obedient to duty, continued to obey orders and to stumble along the road in the dark, scarcely conscious of what was happening. During the night, when a stallion broke loose and ran down the road with a fence rail tied to the bridle rein, the men thought the enemy was attacking and for some minutes they fired at one another.

Lee himself had a strange experience. An officer of General Gordon's staff brought him two letters which had been found that evening on one of a couple of Federal spies captured in Confederate uniform. The letters showed that General Grant himself was at Jetersville and that the Federal infantry who had been farthest from Petersburg at the beginning of the retreat were close now on the heels of the Confederates. Lee was so much absorbed in this news that he was slow to answer a question General Gordon had sent by the staff officer: Should the two spies be shot at once, or should they be held as prisoners. Lee said: "Tell the General the lives of so many of our men are at stake that all my thoughts must now be given to them. Let him keep the prisoners until he hears further from me." Afterward, some of Lee's officers thought the General said this because he felt that the end of the war was near and that he should not kill men, even spies, when their death would not help the Southern cause.

Lee rode on the 6th of April with the troops of the First Corps who led the retreat. This place in the column he chose because he knew that if the Army was to escape, it had to push steadily on. He must be where he could make prompt decision if the route had to be changed. All the troops could move faster if he were at the front. His veterans responded to his presence. Tired as were the troops of Longstreet, they kept to the road and, in early afternoon, reached the Southside Railroad at Rice Station, about six miles southeast of Farmville. At Rice, Lee hailed the column until the rear Divisions caught up.

After Field's Division and that of Mahone had arrived, there was a much longer wait than Lee had expected. Lee took advantage of this delay to make an examination of the high ground that overlooked a little stream of two arms, known as Sayler's Creek. Across the lower stretch of the creek, on a distant hill, Lee saw white objects he could not identify. He said to an officer who arrived at the moment, "Captain, are those sheep or not?"

The young man looked. "No, General," he said, "they are Yankee wagons."

Lee put his field glasses to his eyes. "You are right," he answered, "but what are they doing there?" If any wagon train should be in that position, it should be Confederate: Why were Federals so far around in that direction? What had happened? Had disaster occurred? To ascertain, Lee rode back toward Rice but stopped on the way to talk briefly with General Mahone. Suddenly Colonel Venable, one of Lee's staff officers, rode up and asked if Lee had received his message.

"No," Lee answered.

The Federals, Colonel Venable sadly reported, had captured all the Confederate wagons between the two branches of Sayler's Creek. To lose the wagons was terrible, but the infantry? Had anything been heard of the Generals whose troops were behind Longstreet? The Colonel had heard nothing. In a few terse words Lee directed Mahone to move his Division back toward the Creek, and he rode with the commander of these troops to a crest that overlooked part of the nearer valley. The moment he arrived, Lee drew rein and gasped, because he saw below him, as Mahone said afterwards, "hurrying teamsters with their teams and dangling traces (no wagons), retreating infantry without hats, a harmless mob, with the massive columns of the enemy moving orderly on."

Lee straightened himself and exclaimed, "My God! Has the Army dissolved?" A moment later, he took a battleflag from a passing colorbearer and rode out to rally the men. They proved to be survivors of Divisions on which powerful Federal forces had closed from front and from rear. Exhausted Confederate officers had failed to give the correct orders. Confusion had followed. After a brief, futile battle, most of the troops of Anderson and of Ewell had surrendered. Part of the Army under General Gordon had taken the wrong turn on the road and met overwhelming Federals. In the two phases of the Battle of Sayler's Creek, about a third of the Confederate Army was captured.

With those of his men who still had strength enough to march, Lee moved westward again that night and about daylight on the 7th of April reached the town of Farmville. There, at last, abundant food was waiting on trains that had been sent down from Lynchburg on the Southside Railroad. With relief that could not be put into words, the leading troops received the first bread and meat some of them had seen since they had consumed the last of their rations four days previously. These soldiers eagerly seized their rations and moved to the north of the Appomattox River. There they thought they would be free to cook their food and would be safe for the day. All the bridges across the river were supposed to have been destroyed.

Fate would not have it so. The half-dead men were frying their bacon and cooking bread when Lee received news that shook his masterful poise. Through somebody's blunder—nobody knew whose— one of the bridges had not been burned. Strong Federal troops already were in close pursuit north of the river. The Confederates had to grab up their uncooked meat and dough, or throw it away, and run for their stacked rifles. Thousands of men got nothing to eat. The starving Army had to retreat once more.

CHAPTER TWENTY-ONE

The End of Lee's Battles

B
Y THE EVENING of the 7th of April, Lee had with him only the strongest and the most resolute of his soldiers. Many of the bravest had dropped from exhaustion. Other devoted men had dragged themselves along but reluctantly had thrown away the rifles they no longer could carry. The few cowards and some of the feeble of heart had crept away in the darkness to beg, to steal or to surrender. Starved horses were breaking down along with the men. Everywhere on the highway that led to Lynchburg, vehicles and dying animals littered the road. When possible, the loaded wagons were set afire to keep their contents from falling into the hands of the enemy. Pale, staggering men looked like ghosts where their faces were lighted by the flames.

If General Lee knew by this time that the end had come, he told nobody. He was weary and burdened but outwardly he was calm and almost as confident in appearance as if he still felt sure the Army would escape and join Johnston in the successful continuance of the war. On the 8th of April, conditions made thousands think the General would pull them out of the trap the Federals were trying to spring. The march that morning was not interrupted by Union pursuit. Spring sunshine was bright. Scarcely a shot was heard. The cavalry reported that the blue infantry were behind them. Indications there were, also, that the Federals were moving westward parallel to the Confederates and South of them. Of course, if this parallel column marched faster than Lee's Army could, then the Unionists might cut off the retreat, just as they had at Jetersville. If the Federals did *not* head off the retreat, all still would come out right as the boys so often had said when they had talked of General Lee's outwitting the enemy.

On the evening of the 8th, the Army halted on the nearer side of a little stream close to Appomattox Court House. It was a humble countryside, untroubled by war. The road was ugly and deeply washed, but the pines had the lustrous green of new life. The tall oaks were tasseling. If there had been rations, the men might have rested in hope. Even as it was, at sunset they were not wholly in despair.

After nightfall there was a difference for those soldiers on high ground. North of them the clouds shone gray. Eastward, there was a red reflection in the sky—Federal campfires! In the South, it was the same. Almost the whole of that arc of the horizon was red from the fires the far-extended Union Divisions had lighted. Eagerly, anxiously, heart in mouth, observers looked westward, up the road to Lynchburg. There, too, the Confederates saw the ominous glow of fires. They were not so numerous as in the South and in the West, but the red was there! Federals in unknown numbers were across the road. On three sides, the Army was surrounded. The only escape was northward, in the direction that would carry the Army into a land made barren by war.

At his camp in the woods, Lee met with his senior lieutenants to decide what should be done. The day before he had received under flag of truce a letter in which Grant had called for the surrender of the Army. Lee had shown this to no one except Longstreet whose only comment had been, "Not yet." In an answer to the Federal commander, Lee had inquired what terms would be offered. Grant had said in a second letter that he would insist on no terms except the surrender of the men and their pledge not to fight again until they were ex-

changed. Lee's reply had carried his refusal to surrender but had
suggested a meeting for a general consideration of peace. No answer
to this letter had been received. In the absence of any further word
from Grant, the fate of the Army hung on its ability to cut its way
through the Federals who were across the road to Lynchburg. That,
in turn, depended on how strong the Federals were and whether they
were cavalry or infantry. A light force of cavalry could be swept aside,
but if a heavy force of infantry was encountered, then nothing remained for Lee to do except . . . to surrender.

Plans were made for Gordon's infantry and Fitz Lee's cavalry to
attack in front the next morning. Behind these troops, the rest of the
Army was to proceed with few wagons and guns so that the column,
if it got away, could move fast. All this was arranged by General Lee
who then laid down for a few hours of rest.

About 3 o'clock Lee arose, dressed himself in his best uniform, tied
his officer's red sash around his waist, and put on his finest sword.
When asked later in the morning why he did this, he said simply: "I
have probably to be General Grant's prisoner and thought I must make
my best appearance." Astride Traveller, he rose to the front and soon
heard the guns of Gordon's attack. The fire swelled and dwindled and
rose again and then continued unevenly. From the sound Lee could
not tell whether Gordon was gaining or losing ground. Consequently
an officer was sent forward to get a report. It was 8 o'clock when the
officer came back with this message from Gordon: "Tell General Lee
I have fought my Corps to a frazzle, and I fear I can do nothing unless
I am heavily supported by Longstreet's Corps." Gordon had met both
infantry and cavalry in large numbers. These Federals had beaten off
his attack and now were trying to get between him and the other
Confederate troops. Longstreet could not help. His small force was
facing a great mass of Unionists who were closing from the rear.

To the report of this situation, Lee listened in silence. A moment later he said in anguish of spirit: "Then there is nothing left for me to do but to go and see General Grant, and I would rather die a thousand deaths."

His words were heard by numbers of his officers. For a minute or two they were overwhelmed with grief. "Oh, General," one of them broke out, "what will history say of the surrender of the Army in the field?"

"Yes," Lee replied, "I know they will say hard things of us." He went on: "They will not understand how we were overwhelmed by numbers. But that is not the question, Colonel: The question is, is it right to surrender this Army. If it is right, then I will take all the responsibility."

Consciousness of this duty strengthened him for a short while, but soon he looked across the field toward the Federal position and said, as if to himself, "How easily I could be rid of this, and be at rest! I have only to ride along the line and all will be over!" He paused and took a grip on his emotions: "But it is our duty to live. What will become of the women and children of the South if we are not here to protect them?"

He talked next with Longstreet and Mahone and found that they believed he should surrender, but one of the younger Generals, Porter Alexander, said he thought the Army should scatter and take to the woods and reassemble later. Two-thirds of the men, Alexander argued, could get away.

Lee answered that the number was too small to accomplish anything. After explaining that, Lee continued: "Then, General, you and I as Christian men have no right to consider only how this would affect us. We must consider the effect on the country as a whole. Already it is demoralized by the four years of war. If I took your advice, then men would be without rations and under no control of officers. They would become mere bands of marauders, and the enemy's cavalry would pursue them and overrun many sections they may never have occasion to visit. We would bring on a state of affairs it would take the country years to recover from. And, as for myself, you young fellows might go to bushwhacking, but the only dignified course for me would be to go to General Grant and surrender myself and take the consequences of my acts."

In that spirit Lee rode to the rear, where he hoped Grant would meet him for the conference he had suggested the previous day. Instead, Grant sent word that he could not consider a general peace. Lee learned, also, that the powerful Union troops in rear of Longstreet had orders to advance and did not think they could wait for a further message to be sent General Grant. After several exchanges, the Northern officers agreed to a brief truce in order to permit Lee to dispatch a letter to the Federal commander. As Grant was believed to be on a road South of the Confederates, Lee was told that he might save time by having the paper carried to the front. Lee accordingly wrote a brief note in which he asked an interview.

While this message was being forwarded to Grant, there was a long, long wait under a tree in a small apple orchard by the side of the Lynchburg road. Lee had little to say. His companions did not attempt to talk to him because they understood how he was suffering. About 12:15, he saw a Federal officer coming down the road from the direction of Appomattox. With him was a Confederate. Everyone made the same guess: The man in blue brought a letter from Grant.

"General," said Longstreet, "unless he offers us honorable terms, come back and let us fight it out."

Lee made no answer, but Longstreet thought his chief looked firmer because of the advice. Quickly Lee read the letter from his opponent. It was an offer to meet Lee at any place the Confederate leader named. The preliminaries were ended; the time had come for the final act. It could be nothing less than the surrender of that gallant Army of devoted men. The thought was agonizing; the very word "surrender" was one that burnt any Southern lips that uttered it; but it had to be spoken.

With the Federal officer, a member of his own staff and a courier, Lee rode down to the little stream, where Traveller stopped for a long drink, and then he rode up the slight grade and into the village. Another wait there was while Lee's staff officer, Col. Charles Marshall, searched for a house in which to hold the meeting with Grant. The final choice was the two-story frame dwelling of Maj. Wilmer McLean who, by the strangest of chances, had moved from Manassas after the battle of July 21, 1861, and had come to Appomattox to escape all contact with war.

Lee rode into the yard of the McLean house, dismounted, climbed the steps, went into the parlor and took a seat near a table in the front, farther corner of the room. There he remained for half-an-hour, a terrible half hour of silence that must have seemed as long as a lifetime of misery. Then, from the road, came the clatter of horses' hoofs and the sound of many boots on the steps. Soon a thin, slightly stooped and bearded man of middle height walked into the room. It was Grant. He shook hands quietly. Then he sat down at a table in the middle of the room and spoke briefly to the staff officer who had accompanied him. The officer stepped out and came back in a moment with a dozen or more bluecoated Generals and Colonels, who silently lined the wall. These were Grant's lieutenants. He wanted them to be present at the death of the Army they had helped to kill.

There was a brief reference by the two leaders to the fact that they had been in Mexico at the same time. After a tense pause, Lee began: "I suppose, General Grant, that the object of our meeting is fully understood. I asked to see you to ascertain upon what terms you would receive the surrender of my Army." This was said with perfect courage and with flawless self-command, though everyone knew that Lee would have given his life to be spared the necessity of uttering those few words.

Grant was as courteous and considerate as a man could be. Not one note of exultation was in his answer; not one glance did he turn to the other officers, whose hearts were beating high. The Federal commander said simply that he would accept the surrender of the Army, would leave the officers their swords, and would let the men go to their homes. All arms, animals and equipment must be given up.

When these generous terms were written out, Lee explained that in the Confederate Army the cavalrymen and some of the artillerists owned their horses. Would these men be permitted to take their animals? Grant reflected. He did not know, he said, that any of Lee's troops owned their horses, but he supposed most of the soldiers were small farmers who might not be able to raise a crop to carry them through the next winter unless they had their horses. "I will arrange it this way: I will not change the terms as now written, but I will instruct the officers I shall appoint to receive the paroles to let all the men who claim to own a horse or mule take the animals home with them to work their little farms."

Lee's face showed his relief: "This," he said, "will have the very best possible effect upon the men; it will be very gratifying and will do much toward conciliating our people."

One other painful explanation Lee was compelled to make: He had Federal prisoners he could not feed; in fact, he had no provisions for his own men, and he hoped Grant would permit the use of rations ordered from Lynchburg. Lee was ignorant of it, but these trains containing the food already had been captured. Grant did not humiliate Lee by announcing it. He merely said he would send rations to Lee's men but unfortunately had no forage for the horses.

In a few minutes, the terms of surrender were copied. Lee's acceptance was written by Colonel Marshall and was signed by the General. After a few more words, Lee rose, shook hands with Grant, bowed to the other officers and left the room. While waiting for his horse, he stood on the porch and, when he put on his gauntlets, he abstractedly smote his hands together as he looked across the fields to the hill where the remnant of his Army waited. Soon the horse was ready. Lee mounted. On the porch Grant and the other Federals took off their hats. Lee raised his without a word and rode slowly off.

The early halt in the fighting that day and the passage of the flags of truce had led some of the soldiers to suspect that a surrender was being arranged. Most of the higher officers knew this was true. Thousands of other Confederates had never admitted even to themselves the possibility of such a thing. Now, as they saw Lee coming up the road, they went to meet him. Anxious, doubtful, curious or confident, they crowded around the General, who steeled himself for the ordeal. The men started to cheer him, and then, when they saw in his face the agony of his spirit, they sensed the reason for it and choked their cheer. "General," some of them asked, "are we surrendered?" Others in startled voices repeated the inquiry. As they spoke, they closed around him in the road and took off their caps. He removed his hat and bowed, but he could make no answer. Still the question, "General, General, are we surrendered?" Painfully, Lee pulled in his horse and stopped in the midst of the throng. In shaken tones, struggling with his emotions, he said slowly: "Men we have fought the war together, and I have done the best I could for you. You will all be paroled and go to your homes until exchanged." He tried to say more but all he could force from his trembling lips was a half-inaudible "Good-bye."

His misery made the soldiers forget theirs. They crowded even closer around him again as he started onward. Some stretched out trembling hands to him; some touched his arm, his uniform, his boots, his horse, and they gave him such comfort as they could. "General, we'll fight yet; General, say the word and we'll go in and fight 'em yet." When he reached the apple orchard, they came as close as the guards would permit and, later, when he rode back to his tent in the woods they followed him there, with blessings, with tears, with pledges and with appeals that he lead them once more against the enemy.

Rations came to some of the Confederate camps that night, and to others the next day. Rolls were made of the soldiers who remained to the last. Paroles were printed. All the details were arranged in exact accord with the terms Lee and Grant had signed. By Lee's direction an address was prepared and was read to all his troops. In this famous "General Order No. 9" or "last order," Lee told the men that he had not surrendered them because he doubted their willingness to fight but because "valor and devotion could accomplish nothing that could compensate for the loss that must have attended the continuance of the contest." Terms of surrender were explained again. The concluding words were these: "You will take with you the satisfaction that proceeds from the consciousness of duty faithfully performed; and I earnestly pray that a Merciful God will extend to you His blessing and protection. With an unceasing admiration of your constancy and devotion to your country, and a grateful remembrance of your kind and generous consideration for myself, I bid you all an affectionate farewell."

To this tribute, the Federals added that of their considerate silence. They were as splendid as brave men could be in sparing the feelings of a defeated adversary; but their commander insisted that formal surrender be made. The Northern people must have evidence that the most dreaded "rebel" Army had laid down its arms and its flags in front of a Federal line. On the 11th, the artillerymen yielded up their guns.

The next morning, the Confederate infantry came down the hill, crossed the little river and marched between the open ranks of Union troops who chivalrously saluted them. So few were the survivors that their battleflags were crowded together until the heads of all the men appeared to be under the red halo of their banners.

CHAPTER TWENTY-TWO

A Dedication to Peace and Labor

UNTIL HIS MEN made that last march under their hallowed flags, General Lee remained near them. As they were surrendering their arms and their banners, he was starting to Richmond, where Mrs. Lee and his daughters had spent the winter. When he reached the captured, prostrate city on the afternoon of April 15, he was weary, heavy of heart, and in acutest need of quiet and rest. For a few days he slept long hours. While awake he sat silently in his room or with Mrs. Lee. He found her much shaken and embittered by the war but full of courage. About a week after the General's return, Mrs. Lee wrote: "I feel that I could have blessed God if those who were prepared had filled a soldier's grave. [Now] I bless Him that they are spared, I trust for future usefulness to their unhappy country. . . . For my part, it will always be a source of pride and consolation to me to know that all mine have perilled their lives, fortunes and even fame in so holy a cause."

By the time the General was sufficiently rested for his mind to act with its full vigor, he was ready to make the first of the decisions by which he was guided for the remainder of his life. He knew better than did almost anyone else in the South that further resistance was futile after the surrender of the Army of Northern Virginia. The results of the conflict had to be accepted, and they could be accepted the more readily by him because he had never indulged in hate during the war. He felt, also, in spite of his deep modesty, that he had performed his full duty. A remark made by him at a later time undoubtedly reflected his feelings in May, 1865. To a gentleman who mourned over the misery of the people, Lee said: "Yes, all that is very sad, and might be a cause of self-reproach but that we are conscious that we have humbly tried to do our duty. We may, therefore, with calm satisfaction, trust in God and leave results with Him."

This did not mean that he shut his eyes to the wretchedness of the South. Its railroads were almost ruined. Bridges were destroyed. Because no mail could be delivered, little business could be transacted. The currency of the South had lost its value completely. No patriotic Southerner had any buying power. Few had any work. Thousands of families had lost their wage-earners. Poverty and desolation were upon the land. General Lee saw all this and agonized over it, but he did not think the paroled Confederates should sit in the ashes of their cities and weep over their woes. The young men must not despair. They must stay in the South, accept such work as they could find, and take part in public affairs. Veterans who could not get other employment should go to farms where at least they could earn their bread. In a letter to one of his staff officers Lee said: "Tell [our returning soldiers] they must all set to work, and if they cannot do what they prefer, do what they can. Virginia wants all their aid, all their support, and the presence of all her sons to sustain and recuperate her. They must therefore put themselves in a position to take part in her government, and not to be deterred by obstacles in their way. There is much to be done which they only can do."

From the first, Lee had to combat in the hearts of some of his people a bitterness that might lead to lasting hate of the victorious Union. He soon saw how far the spirit of vengeance was going to lead Northern "Radicals," as they were called, but he felt that argument and dispute merely would aggravate the evils these extremists would impose on the South. In the first months after the close of the war, Lee scarcely would mention the conflict, except to praise the devotion of the soldiers. "All should unite," he said, "in honest efforts to obliterate the effects of war, and to restore the blessings of peace." This was the duty of the young people, he thought, as well as of their parents. One day not long after his return from Appomattox, he heard angry shouts from the street and the sobs of a hurt child. The General rushed out and found that some of the youngsters of the neighborhood were beating a Northern boy whom they had encountered. Lee made them stop pummeling the newcomer and in earnest tones he rebuked them for attacking a lad who had never done them any harm. As Virginia gentlemen, he said, they ought to treat a stranger kindly even though he was a Northerner. With that, the General took the youth into the house and kept him there till the gang had gone away.

This courageous acceptance of the results of the war, while hearts still burned with the fire of battle, prompted General Lee to take an even more positive stand. His old opponent, General George Meade, called to see him while the Army of the Potomac were passing through Richmond. With the candor of one who had been a friend for many years before the war, Meade urged Lee to take the oath of allegiance to the United States. If Lee did this, said Meade, he would influence other Confederates to do the same thing. That would promote reunion. Lee explained that difficulties stood in the way at the time, but after his meeting with Meade, he found conditions quickly changed. On May 29, President Andrew Johnson issued a proclamation in which he said that participation in the "rebellion" would be forgiven all Southerners outside of fourteen specified classes of persons. This was of great importance because it meant that soldiers who received this so-called amnesty or general pardon could hope to share again in the government of their state. General Lee came within the fourteen classes excepted from the amnesty, but the proclamation authorized a person in any of these classes to make written application for individual pardon. Lee decided he ought to do this. The one thing that seemed to stand in his way was that a few hotheaded, venomous men threatened to have him convicted of treason and hanged. He thought that if he applied for pardon, some might think he was seeking to evade responsibility for what he had done. After thinking this over, Lee wrote Grant a letter in which he said that if he were to be called to trial, he was ready. If he was not to be arraigned, he wished to apply for pardon.

This act on General Lee's part was approved and emulated by many Southerners. They decided that the example of their leader was one they could follow without humiliation or dishonor. Other Southerners thought Lee had gone too far. General Grant forwarded to the President the application for pardon and insisted that a man who had been given a parole as a prisoner of war was protected by that document from arrest for acts performed during the war. Largely because of Grant's stand, Lee was not brought into court but neither was he granted a pardon.

All this happened during April, May and the first half of June, 1865. Lee stayed in Richmond somewhat unwillingly during these ten weeks, except for one brief visit to kinspeople in a nearby county. He was anxious to leave the city and to go to work to earn a living for his wife and daughters, but he had not been tendered, as yet, any position he could accept.

Offers of almost every kind of bounty and of gift came to him. A rich Britisher wrote to say he would be honored to place an English estate and a regular income at General Lee's disposal for life. "I am deeply grateful," Lee replied, "[but] I cannot desert my native State in the hour of her adversity." Lee's own people, from their devotion to him, tried to get him to share the little they possessed. One of the members of the old cavalry regiment he had commanded in Texas came to the house in Richmond with a great basket of food. The man had served in the Union Army during the war, but, he explained, he had purchased the provisions because he had heard Lee was in distress. Before the old trooper left, he cried: "Good-bye, Colonel! God bless you! If I could have got over in time I would have been with ye!"

Another call at Lee's house in Richmond was remembered by him to his last day. Two ragged Confederates rang the door bell and asked to see the General. He found it difficult to receive all visitors but he seldom could deny himself to his own men. When he entered the parlor and shook hands with the soldiers, they told him they spoke for about sixty of their comrades who were too dirty to enter a private house. All of these men were landowners in the same remote mountain community, which they believed to be safe from any Federal raid. They had been told that General Lee was in danger of arrest and trial. If he would come with them, they would provide him a home, would work for him, and would fight for him if the Federals attempted to seize him. Lee was deeply moved, but he answered: "You would not have your General run away and hide. He must stay here and meet his fate." They were reluctant to accept his refusal, though he thanked them with more feeling than he usually let himself show. Before they departed, he gave the tattered men a few garments from his own scanty wardrobe.

Grateful as Lee was for such kindnesses as his old soldiers and the people of Richmond showered on him, he did not feel that he should remain idle or subject his invalid wife to the strain of endless visitors. If he found no salaried position, he must buy a farm and move to it. While he was in the first stage of looking for a suitable place, he and

LEE IN LATER YEARS

Photo courtesy of Mrs. Blair Stringfellow and Dementi Studio, Richmond

Mrs. Lee received from a wealthy widow, Mrs. Elizabeth Randolph Cocke, an invitation to occupy as long as they would a house on her James River estate above Richmond. The dwelling was not elaborate but it was adequate and it was away from crowds. Mrs. Cocke soon came down to Richmond to press her invitation and to describe to Mrs. Lee the arrangements that could be made. So generously and kindly did Mrs. Cocke explain everything that the Lees accepted. Before the end of June, the family left Richmond by packet boat on the canal that ran along the left bank of James River. The next day they were at Oakland, the home of Mrs. Cocke. After a restful week there, they moved to the smaller property, Derwent, which was furnished simply but comfortably.

In the quiet of the countryside, where visitors were few and always considerate, rest and reflection raised the spirits of General Lee. He remained at the house or in the yard much of the time, but every day when the weather was favorable, he rode Traveller. During the war he had made it his mental rule to think of pleasant things only while he was taking his exercise out of doors. This habit of thought had become fixed and it always made a ride or a walk a renewal of strength.

At Derwent, too, for the first time, Lee permitted himself to think again of the battles he had fought. He did not review them in any spirit of personal pride. That was not his nature. His pride was in what the men of his small Army had accomplished with their poor guns and gear against their more numerous, perfectly equipped Northern adversaries. As Lee reflected on what his soldiers had done, he concluded that he ought to write a history of the campaigns of the Army of Northern Virginia. "This," said he, "is the only tribute that can now be paid to the worth of [the Army's] noble officers and soldiers."

During mid-summer, 1865, then, it appeared that General Lee

would live the retired life of a farmer and would confine his public service to writing this history. In addition, he would quietly work for reconciliation and would oppose every evil influence that might keep Southerners from working for the recovery of the country. That would be the measure of Lee's last years. So almost anyone would have said until that August day when a tall, bulky gentleman rode up at the lane at Derwent and introduced himself as John W. Brockenbrough of Lexington, Virginia.

General Lee had never seen Judge Brockenbrough and he had no idea of the gentleman's purpose in visiting him. In a few minutes he found that the Judge had come to ask of him a decision that might change all his plans. Mr. Brockenbrough was rector of Washington College, Lexington, and he had ridden from the Shenandoah Valley to announce that at a meeting on the 4th of August, the trustees unanimously had elected General Lee president of the institution. The salary was $1,500 a year; a house and ground for a garden would be supplied. In addition, the president, who usually taught philosophy, would receive one-fifth of the tuition fees of the students. After explaining all this, Judge Brockenbrough expressed most earnestly the hope that Lee would accept.

A college presidency! Lee had not been happy in his only previous experience of that sort as Superintendent of the United States Military Academy. So far as is known, he never had considered such a position as a possibility after the war. He knew he could not teach philosophy and he doubted whether he was fitted in other respects for the position. Besides, he was hated by many Northerners and often was denounced in newspapers and magazines as a "traitor" and the most dangerous of all the "rebels." A college that needed money might be hampered in asking for funds in the North if he were its executive.

All that Lee would promise Judge Brockenbrough was that he would consider the offer. After the visitor left, the General gave long and earnest thought to the proposal and finally went to see a nearby friend, Rev. Joseph P. B. Wilmer, who had been chaplain at the University of Virginia and also the United States Navy before the war. Dr. Wilmer was surprised and not pleased to hear that Lee was even considering the presidency of so poor and feeble a college as that at Lexington. If the General were willing to head an institution of learning, said Wilmer, any one of numerous strong and distinguished universities would be proud to have him as president. Apparently Lee had not regarded the strength or weakness, the wealth or poverty of Washington College as a reason for or against acceptance. He merely told Wilmer that Providence seemed to have opened to him that door, and not another. What he wished to ascertain from Wilmer was whether, in plain words, he was competent to direct the college. In the event he was, he was willing to devote the remaining years of his life to the school at Lexington in the hope that he could help the South and its young men.

Wilmer, of course, told the General that he was wholly qualified to direct an educational establishment and that there was no finer work than that of giving colleges the spirit of Christianity. Reassured by this, General Lee on the 24th of August wrote Judge Brockenbrough and the committee. He explained that he could not undertake more than the general direction of the institution. Next he reminded the committee he was "an object of censure to a portion of the Country" and might on that account "draw upon the college a feeling of hostility." Then followed these words: "I think it is the duty of every citizen, in the present condition of the Country, to do all in his power to aid in the restoration of peace and harmony, and in no way to oppose the policy of the State or General Government directed to that end. It is particularly incumbent on those charged with the instruction of the youth of the country to set them an example of submission to authority, and I could not consent to be the subject of animadversion upon the College." He concluded that if the trustees took the view that his services would "be advantageous to the College and Country" he would accept. Otherwise he would have to decline.

The trustees, of course, believed that Lee's acceptance would mean large service to the South and new life to the college. They made arrangements for the teaching of philosophy by a member of the faculty and they did everything possible, considering the poverty of the times, to facilitate the work and increase the comfort of the new president. The published announcement of Lee's acceptance quoted what he had said in his letter of acceptance, concerning the duty of working for peace and harmony. "In dedicating his future life to the holy work of educating the youth of his country," the trustees added, "General Lee presents a new and interesting phase of his grand and heroic character . . ."

Lee himself said nothing publicly, but in private he adhered steadfastly to the code of conduct he had outlined to the trustees. In his answers to many letters from former soldiers, seamen, and political leaders, he dwelt often and earnestly on the duty of reconciliation. To a magazine editor he wrote: "It should be the object of all to avoid controversy, to allay passions, give full scope to reason and every kindly feeling. By doing this and encouraging our citizens to engage in the duties of life with all their heart and mind, with a determination not to be turned aside by thoughts of the past and fears of the future, our country will not only be restored in material prosperity, but will be advanced in science, in virtue and in religion."

In that spirit, on September 15, 1865, he saddled his old war horse

Traveller and started for his new post. Few there were who realized at the time what it meant to the South for the most venerated of her living sons to take "the road from Appomattox to Lexington," the road from civil contention to the wiser and wider education of the Confederates, their younger brothers, their sons, and their sons' sons.

CHAPTER TWENTY-THREE

Lee Sees a Reviving Southern Life

WHEN GENERAL LEE reached Lexington, he found Washington
College barely alive. Nothing but the energy of a few trustees
and the devotion of the members of its small faculty had saved it from
death. Buildings were in such disrepair that the opening of the session had to be delayed until rooms could be made habitable for
students. The trustees had been compelled to borrow money to meet
the first costs of operations. Such scientific apparatus as the college
had possessed before the war had been destroyed or carried away.
Nearly all the books of the Library had been scattered. Some of the
buildings were being used by the Federal garrison of the town. On
part of the campus, field crops were growing.

Trustees, faculty and townspeople supported General Lee in efforts
that quickly gave the college a vigor it probably had never known
before. Although only fifty students registered on the scheduled date
of opening, others soon came. Young men continued to arrive all
through the first session until the enrolment reached 146. Three members were added to the faculty. Gifts that were generous for the time
encouraged hope that the college would have a sufficient endowment
to provide new courses the faculty suggested and Lee approved.

At first the work burdened the General. The closest economy was
required in the smallest items. Careful always in his own expenditures,
Lee was even more vigilant in directing the finances of the college. He

had so little help in his office that he had to write in person most of the letters to parents and inquirers. With his own pen, also, he tried to reply to the many personal communications he received. Officers wrote for recommendations; former soldiers and their wives sought his counsel; needy persons addressed begging letters to him; strangers asked for interviews. Lee never had liked paper work as the old army was wont to style it, but he felt he had to do it now and he made no complaint. The hardest of work was a patriotic ideal.

Another ideal he set for himself was that of knowing every student and the academic record and problems of each of them. He soon found that the men fell into three categories. First were those, few in number, who had fought in his Army and had come to college because they had a little money and did not know what vocation to follow. Some of these were ex-soldiers old enough to wear beards. They spent more time in pool rooms and bars than in the class rooms and they seldom remained for many months in the quiet little Valley town. A much larger element of Lee's veterans in the student body was intensely interested in making careers and consequently caused no trouble. The third group was composed of younger boys of the type that normally would be entering college. These students, most of them freshmen, were known to the former soldiers as "yearlings."

General Lee never "lectured" these men or "preached" to them at chapel, but he tried to get them to live according to a few spiritual laws which he knew from his own experience were sound. "As a general principle," he told a professor, "you should not force young men to do their duty, but let them do it voluntarily and thereby develop their character." When a new student asked for a copy of the rules, Lee said: "We have no printed rules. We have but one rule here, and it is that every student must be a gentleman." This did not imply that students could act as they pleased. They were expected, on the contrary, to study diligently and to do the tasks assigned them as a matter of duty and of self-discipline. One of the General's favorite maxims was, "Obedience to lawful authority is the foundation of manly character." He sometimes stated it another way: "You cannot be a true man until you learn to obey."

If a boy did too much work, the General admonished him. One day he called to his office a brilliant student named Milton Humphreys and told the young man not to overwork himself.

"I am so impatient," Humphreys explained, "to make up for the time I lost in the army—"

Lee let him get no further. "Mr. Humphreys," he said, almost wrathfully, "however long you live and whatever you accomplish, you will find that the time you spent in the Confederate Army was the most profitably spent portion of your life. Never again speak of having 'lost time' in the army!"

The boy who went to the other extreme received exhortation, warning and, sometimes, a little mild sarcasm. To the surprise of a lazy collegian, the General asked him one day: "How is your mother?" Before the puzzled student could say anything, Lee added: "I am sure you must be devoted to her; you are so careful of the health of her son." In every instance, the treatment was shaped, as far as Lee could, to the individual student. "I always respect persons," he said to a professor who was arguing for adherence to what had been done in a similar case, "and care little for precedent." To a new teacher he said: "May I give you one piece of advice? . . . Always observe the stage-driver's rule . . . Always take care of the poor horses."

By the end of the second session, Lee had 399 students under his care. To help them and to advance the college, he had to continue his hard work and to adhere to an exact schedule. That long had been his practice. It now was his inflexible, time-saving rule. He always at-

Photo by Wayne Andrews

CAMPUS OF WASHINGTON COLLEGE

NOW WASHINGTON & LEE UNIVERSITY

tended chapel in the morning, then went to his office and remained there all the forenoon, or else he attended to duties elsewhere on the college campus. In the afternoon he usually would take a ride on Traveller. He retired early because he had found, he said, that "one hour's sleep before midnight is worth two after that time."

On Sunday, the General's schedule was different in detail but was as rigid as on weekday. By example and appeal, he tried to get all the students to go on the Sabbath to the church of their choice. Most of them attended the Presbyterian Church, whose minister, Dr. Pratt, had a daughter named Grace. When the rector of the Episcopal Church remarked that the students were going to Dr. Pratt's because of that minister's eloquence, Lee shook his head: "I rather think," he said, "that the attraction is not so much Dr. Pratt's eloquence as it is Dr. Pratt's Grace."

Those students who did go to the Episcopal Church had one diversion to compensate for their failure to see Miss Pratt. The interesting McDonald family of boys, sons of dead Col. Angus McDonald, flocked to that church. Inasmuch as they overflowed their pew, the surplus McDonalds sat on a long bench that ran at right angles to the pews. As the rector was somewhat long-winded in his sermons, one or another of the McDonalds would lose interest, would begin to nod and then presently would fall "cu-thump" to the floor. This occurred every Sunday, in plain sight and with so much regularity that some members of the congregation would watch expectantly to see which of the boys fell first. General Lee never looked aside or even changed expression when the nodding McDonald dropped to the floor.

During the summer, General Lee would go with Mrs. Lee and some of his daughters to one or another of the nearby Springs where hotels sheltered persons of social tastes and invalids who came to "take the water." Occasionally General Custis Lee, the oldest son would go with the family and would afford his father a pleasant, perennial theme of jest. The father never joked about marriage for his daughters and sometimes he seemed to discourage the suggestion that they might find husbands. None of them, in fact, ever married. With his sons it was different. The General was always protesting that he must find wives for the younger Lees and many times he jestingly told girls he wished Robert or Custis or Rooney would marry them. Custis was superbly handsome but was incurably a bachelor. He never flirted and he never danced unless he had to do so. "General Custis," one young lady inquired, "why do you not sit down?" He answered: "I am a modest man and for a modest man to have his hands and his feet on his mind at the same time is too much; when I stand, my feet are off my mind, and I have only my hands to attend to."

Once—and surely with his Father's warm approval—Custis did give a girl a rush at the Springs. That was when a freckled-faced Northern girl with a dumpy figure and no beauty whatever appeared in the ball room. For a few nights nobody outside her own little circle paid any attention to her. Then she was identified as the daughter of a man who had been generously and conspicuously kind to Confederate prisoners of war. As soon as Custis Lee found that out, he passed the word to former officers. From that night forward, the freckled-faced girl was the belle of the season. The most famous men at the Springs contended for the honor of escorting her or of dancing with her.

The senior Lee was himself the central figure of the most notable gatherings at the mountain resorts. When none of the women of his family was sick—one or another usually was—he enjoyed the pleasant company. He usually avoided politics and politicians and he continued to shun all discussion of the war. Gradually, too, the project of writing a history of his Army faded into the background of his mind. He had no time for it.

Before the season ended at the Springs, Lee returned to Lexington. Thereafter, for nine months, most of his energies were devoted to the college, which still was growing and was gaining in funds and in students. New courses created new problems for Lee. Immeasurably greater problems were being raised by the triumph of the Radicals in Congress and the passage of the Reconstruction Acts. Southerners who had accepted the result of the war were outraged by these laws, which were passed in order to keep ex-Confederates from voting and from holding office. Southern States became mere "military districts," over which Federal soldiers presided.

Lee shared the universal resentment of these cruel measures but, as always, he sought to keep the mind of Southerners on their task of upbuilding their farms and their industries. Lee wrote General Early: "We shall have to be patient, and suffer for a while at least; and all controversy, I think, will only serve to prolong angry and bitter feelings, and postpone the periods when reason and charity may resume their sway. At present the public mind is not prepared to receive the truth."

To this course, amid vexations, petty persecutions and abuse in the North, Lee consistently held. He was called to Washington and was examined by a Congressional Committee. When an effort was made to bring President Davis to trial for treason, General Lee was summoned as a witness. Radical newspapers and magazines attacked him and the college. He traveled little except when compelled to do so, and even then he doubted whether he should call on friends. "I am now considered such a monster," he wrote, "that I hesitate to darken with my shadow, the doors of those I love best lest I should bring upon them misfortune." In this there was no self-pity. His grief, deep and ceaseless, was for those who had suffered the miseries of war and, as he feared, had not been able to make a new start in life.

The General had this dark view of the woes of the South when he
learned in the autumn of 1867 that his son William H. Fitzhugh
("Rooney") Lee was engaged to Miss Tabb Bolling of Petersburg.
"Rooney's" first wife, Charlotte Wickham, had died during the war,
to the acute distress of all the Lees. They were glad now that "Rooney"
was to marry again and especially that he had followed the wise an-
cestral rule of the family and had chosen a girl of his own station.

The young lovers knew of course that Mrs. Lee could not attend
the wedding but they were insistent that the General should. "Rooney"
wrote an urgent appeal that his father be present. Lee might have
been less reluctant to say yes if the marriage was to be performed at
some quiet place; but he disliked particularly to go to Petersburg because it was associated with the saddest memories of the struggle. The
desperation of his effort to save that city from bombardment and from
suffering had made for it a special place in his sorrow. "Rooney" had
to come in person to Lexington before the General would agree to be
a guest at the ceremonies.

Once he consented, he made careful preparation. He and Mrs. Lee
decided to give their new daughter-in-law a necklace. For himself the
General ordered a new suit of black broadcloth—perhaps the first
woolen outer garments he had bought after the war. All the details of
his travel were arranged with his old military precision. En route to
Petersburg, the General had to stop in Richmond as an unwilling witness in another effort of the Radicals to find an indictment on which
they could try President Davis for treason. This was an unpleasant incident. Everything else that happened in Richmond, before the time
to go to Petersburg was delightful. Old friends showed him endless
kindness. Visitors almost overwhelmed him.

On the afternoon of November 28, 1867, began the ordeal Lee had dreaded. He went to the station of the Richmond and Petersburg Rail-road and got aboard the special car that had been provided for the wedding guests. His sons and his daughter Mildred doubtless were there. All the young people were full of expectancy. In the mind of the General, memory and not expectancy was uppermost. He was go-ing back to Petersburg for the first time since he had left it on the night of April 2, 1865, and he was going over the same railroad he so often had traveled on hurried journeys to consult with President Davis over some new crisis in the short, troubled life of the Confederacy. He sat alone now, silent and sad-faced, as the train stopped at one and another of the stations of bloody name. Here was Drewry's Bluff which the Federal fleet had assailed in 1862 and Beauregard had defended two years later. Yonder, stripped of summer greenery and raw and red, were the earthworks below the station. After that, the train passed the cork of the bottle that had held Butler. Soon the locomotive was approaching the Appomattox. Behind the hill that overlooked the track was Violet Bank, where Army headquarters had been located for anxious months. The brakes were soon applied for the stop at Pocahontas, directly opposite the town. Scarcely had the wheels ceased to turn than there was the crash of music, the stirring notes of the Marseillaise. The band played the whole of that anthem of freedom and then the musicians clambered aboard the train. Slowly the locomotive pulled the train to the Washington Street Station.

When Lee stepped quietly down from the step of the coach, he saw such a multitude of civilians as never before had gathered to welcome him anywhere. Station, street, windows of nearby hotel—all were jammed. Instant cheers rose. Although the band played loudly the tunes Southerners loved, the greetings of the throng almost drowned even the drums. General Mahone was waiting with carriage drawn by four white horses. Only by Lee's insistent appeal were his old soldiers and their friends restrained from unhitching the animals and pulling the carriage to General Mahone's residence.

It was an experience to open the eyes of Lee. The brave old town and its people had put the war behind them. Although little more than two years and a half had passed since the "day of wrath," Petersburg had reversed the lamentation of the prophet, "how doth the city sit solitary, that was full of people." The city that had sat solitary that dreadful night in April, 1865, now was full of people. They had decent clothing on their backs, health in their bearing, hope in their eyes.

Everywhere Lee found the adults smiling, his old soldiers working or celebrating his presence among them, and the children welcoming him with laughing delight. In the homes he visited, at a reception given him, on the streets—always there was the same enthusiasm for him, the same cheerful vitality of a people who had resolved to live. At the wedding supper, Lee escorted into the dining room lovely Anne Banister, 16 years old, who was wearing her first long dress. A new generation was rising. Anne was a symbol of it.

The wedding ceremony was beautiful. Miss Bolling had ten attendants. A like number of handsome young men supported the groom. Most of the notables of that part of Virginia were present. Both the General's unmarried sons were there along with his nephew, Fitz. Petersburg never had celebrated a finer wedding.

Of all the witnesses, none found more pleasure than General Lee. When the time came for him to leave the city, he held, as always, to the schedule he had made, but he admitted that if he had known the young couple were to remain over the week-end in Petersburg, he, too, would have stayed. On his return to Lexington he wrote his son of the delight he had found: ". . . when our armies were in front of

Petersburg, I suffered so much in body and mind on account of the good townspeople, especially on that gloomy night when I was forced to abandon them, that I have always reverted to them in sadness and sorrow. My old feelings returned to me as I passed well-remembered spots and recalled the ravages of the hostile shells. But when I saw the cheerfulness with which the people were working to restore their condition, and witnessed the comforts with which they were surrounded, a load of sorrow which had been pressing upon me for years was lifted from my heart." In the renewed life of his people, he lived anew.

CHAPTER TWENTY-FOUR

"Strike the Tent"

THE SESSION OF 1867–68 brought troubles over a young Northern storekeeper, a former Federal soldier, who asserted that students of Washington College had beaten him and had threatened his life. Several Radical papers took up the incident and made it the basis of new attacks on the South. General Lee punished the few individuals who actually had been involved in the affair, but he could not keep the extremists of the North from telling untruths about the occurrence. He simply had to make the best of it and to do what he could to quiet those of his own people who were aroused by the injustice of the attacks.

All the while, he kept advocating in his quiet way his creed of Southern recovery—work, economy, patience, self-denial, faith. Concerning the gospel of honorable toil, he wrote his kinsman Hill Carter: "Work is what we now require, work by everybody and work especially by white hands. Labor and economy will carry us through. We must spend less . . . than we formerly did. We require very little and we must use that little sparingly. By this course the good old times . . . will return again. We may not see them, but our children will, and we will live over again in them. I hope they may imitate the virtues and avoid the errors of their ancestors . . ."

In economy, the General practiced what he preached. So did the members of the family. None of them complained because they had to live simply. A young official of the college said of the General: "I have seen him in garments which many men of smaller income and far less reputation would have been unwilling to wear . . . Mrs. Lee's usual occupation in the dining room . . . during the evening was mending her husband's and son's underclothing." One day the same winter a young official met a daughter of the General who at that time was "keeping house." She had on her arm a basket of pears the fineness of which the young man remarked. "Yes," said she, "they are nice and I would offer you one; but I have just enough for my dessert tomorrow."

The General gave generously to charities and to the church, but he believed the people who lived after a war had rigidly to save money if they were to replace what had been wasted or destroyed. When Lee violated this rule in even a small thing, the family was surprised. Before Christmas, 1868, he asked his youngest daughter Mildred, who had been sick for some weeks the previous summer, what present she wanted. After the practice of girls, she mentioned the various presents she desired, and, on Christmas, found to her embarrassment that her father had given her *all* of them instead of selecting one from her list. Doubtless the family thought this was the climax of the spoiling to which Mildred had been subjected during her sickness, but they did not fail to remember the incident as most unusual. Their economy and that of the General did not arise from stinginess. All the Lees loved elegance. Most of them spent freely when they thought they could afford to do so. After a war, they believed economy was patriotic duty.

As one expression of faith, religion, too, meant more than ever to the General and to his household during the years at Lexington. He made it his special duty to attend chapel exercises every morning at college and he took an active part in advancing the little Episcopal Church. Ministers of all the denominations represented in the town served successively as chaplain of the college. At home, General Lee always had prayers before breakfast and he much disliked for anyone, guest or member of the family, to be late at these devotions. Before his new daughter-in-law came on her first visit, her husband, "Rooney" Lee, told her of his father's insistence on promptness. Her spirit was challenged. During a stay of three weeks, she did not have a single mark of tardiness charged against her. The result, she said afterward, was that she rose greatly in the General's estimation. Privately she confided to the girls of the household that she did not believe General Lee's idol, George Washington, would have the entire good opinion of Lee if he were late at morning prayers.

Guests were more frequent now, because the trustees insisted on building for General Lee a dwelling which he always was careful to style "The President's residence"—never "my house" or "my home" lest somebody think he regarded it as his personal property. The structure cost something more than $15,000 and was, for the times, a handsome house. In its design was to be seen the General's constant thought of Mrs. Lee. The wide porches and the floor-length windows were designed to make it easy for her rolling-chair to be moved directly from her bedroom out into the light and sunshine. In this residence, which was occupied early in June, 1869, the Lees entertained simply a steady succession of visitors, most of whom were kinspeople or friends of the girls.

Occasionally General Lee had male guests. Some of them thoughtlessly left their shoes outside the door to be polished at night. As the General had no man servant, he cleaned these shoes himself. Often they were muddy because Lexington did not have easy approaches. To get there, a traveler had to use the canal boat, which was slow and excessively uncomfortable, or else he had to take the train to Goshen and come then from the railroad over roads so nearly impassable that the passenger frequently had to get out and walk through the mire. One such visitor asked General Lee which was the better way of getting from Lexington. "It makes but little difference," the General replied, "for whichever route you select, you will wish you had taken the other."

The General's own travel was more frequent now. Besides going to the Springs every summer, he attended in May, 1868, at Lynchburg the council of the Episcopal Church. In April, 1869, he went to Baltimore in the interest of a proposed railroad up the Shenandoah Valley. On his return journey from Baltimore he stopped in Washington and called for a few minutes on President Grant, because he had been told that his old adversary wished him to do so. Their conversation was simple and brief and probably was limited to general remarks on Lee's mission to Baltimore in behalf of the railroad. From Washington, Lee went to Alexandria, which he had not visited since he left it on the 22nd of April, 1861. His reception was as cordial as that given him in Petersburg and was even more personal, because among those who called on him were some who had been his friends and neighbors from boyhood.

It probably was during this brief visit to Alexandria that a young mother brought her child to Lee and asked him to bless it. The General took in his arms the infant that personified, in a sense, the South that he and other devoted men were trying to rebuild from the ashes of war. Lee looked affectionately at the child, murmured perhaps a few words of blessing and returned the infant to the mother. "Madam," said he, "teach him he must deny himself."

That was his message to a new generation in the South. It was delivered when he felt that his own generation was passing. He probably had never been in his full, robust health after his illness in the spring of 1863. The strain of war had been too great for even his strong heart.

He appeared to be better after his return from Alexandria but that probably was because of the satisfaction he had derived from visiting beloved scenes and meeting the friends of youth. When asked if he had enjoyed the trip, he answered, "Very much, but they would make entirely too much fuss over an old rebel." After one of his daughters remarked, later, that he was wearing a hat that should be laid aside, he inquired in mock surprise: "You don't like this hat? Why, I have seen a whole cityful come out to admire it!" Although he spoke with all his old-time cheer, he was actually worse, instead of better and he probably added to the strain by attending the meeting of the Episcopal Council in Fredericksburg. Harder still was another visit to Alexandria in the summer of 1869 for the burial of his brother Smith. At the insistence of his youngest son, Robert, he returned home by way of White House, where Robert was farming. Then the General went in a few days to the Springs but he did not remain there long.

Soon after the opening of the session of 1869–70, the General had an obscure sickness that involved his heart. He managed to get back on his feet within a few days, but he began now to experience some difficulty in breathing when he rode or walked fast. By March, 1870, his condition was so serious that the faculty united in a request that he take a vacation and spend it in travel for the benefit of his health. Reluctantly on the 24th he left Lexington for Florida.

This travel was crowded with so many incidents and covered so great a distance in a time so brief that it undoubtedly injured him physically. Had he not subjected himself to that ordeal he probably would have lived longer; but if a few months more or less of life did not matter greatly, the Southern tour of 1870 had this result: It showed General Lee that popular affection for him was as strong in the Far South as it was in Virginia. Every reception seemed to outdo all the others. His former lieutenants came from afar to do him honor; ex-officers and soldiers brought their children, many of whom were his namesakes. The General was overwhelmed. He declined all requests that he make a speech, but he mingled with the guests at all the receptions and enjoyed meeting them.

The tenderest part of his journey was near the close. From Norfolk he took a steamer up James River, visited the beautiful Brandon estates and went on to Shirley. At the birthplace of his mother, the scene of happy visits of his boyhood days, he met and talked with many of his Carter cousins. One of the younger of them, a witty girl, probably spoke for all of her age and blood when she said: "We regarded him with the greatest veneration. . . . We had heard of God, but here was General Lee!"

From Shirley he went to his sons' plantations again and then to White Marsh, the home in Gloucester County of his cousin Mrs. Prosser Tabb. While he was there, conversation turned to the distress of the South. One of the young women asked in something approaching despair, "What can fate hold for us poor Virginians?"

Lee answered earnestly in words that applied to every Southern State now as then: "You can work for Virginia, to build her up again, to make her great again. You can teach your children to love and cherish her." That was almost his final message to the people with whom he had shared four years of exhausting war: They must work!

From Gloucester he went home by way of Richmond. Afterward he went to Baltimore to consult a renowned physician and on his return he stopped again at Alexandria. When the summer came, he went the rounds of the Springs but found little pleasure or benefit at any of them. Subsequently he went to Staunton to a meeting of the stockholders of the Valley Railroad. There, to his surprise, he was named to the presidency of the company. It was not a position he sought or desired. "It seems to me," he wrote a friend of the college, "that I have already led enough forlorn hopes," but, when told that he and he alone could assure the extension of the railroad to Lexington, he agreed to accept, with the understanding that he would continue as head of the college.

Soon after his election as president of the railroad, the session of 1870–71 opened, the sixth since his coming to Washington College. He attended the opening exercises and met students and faculty in the usual manner. Those who knew him well could see how he was failing in body. To others he seemed merely an old man, though he was not more than 63. His hair was entirely white. He who had been the most erect of men, now stooped slightly. He believed that his end was near but like the young Colonel who had been mortally wounded at Bethesda Church, he was no more afraid to die than he had been to go into the battle.

Quietly if painfully, he did his duty until the 28th of September. That afternoon he went through the rain to a vestry meeting at the church where he presided for more than three hours in the chilly auditorium. His last official act, before adjourning the meeting, was to contribute the sum needed to raise the meagre salary of the rector to a new figure that had been set. From the church, unaccompanied and wrapped only in his military cape—for he never would use an umbrella—Lee walked through the rain to the home where Mrs. Lee had kept supper waiting for him. He took off his cape and went into the dining room.

"You look chilly," said Mrs. Lee.

"Thank you," he answered, "I am warmly clothed."

"You have kept us waiting a long time," Mrs. Lee banteringly said. "Where have you been?"

He made no reply but took his usual place at the head of the table and started to say grace. The words would not come. He tried to speak, hesitated and then sank into his chair.

"Let me pour you out a cup of tea," Mrs. Lee said in alarm, "you look tired."

Again he could say nothing, but a certain look of resignation came into his eyes, as if he knew the end was at hand. Then, carefully and deliberately, he straightened up in his chair just as he had many a time in his saddle when the battle had reached some new crisis of danger or of triumph.

He was placed on a sofa until the doctors could arrive. After they had decided that he had some impairment of circulation, though no paralysis, a bed was set up in the dining room for him. He dozed much of the time that evening but he could move and he roused when any-one spoke to him. The next day he could utter a few words slowly.

All Lexington, all Virginia, the entire South was stirred. One day the news was good; the next it was bad. Often the prediction was made that he would recover; as often men shook their heads sorrow-fully and said that he had had a stroke that would be fatal to him. The General himself took his medicine faithfully and obeyed the doc-tors' orders, but he gave no indication that he expected to get well. A week passed. Then word was whispered that his picture had dropped from the wall. The superstitious said this was an omen. Another night, the sky flashed and shivered with an aurora borealis. A Lexington woman pointed to a passage in Aytoun's "Edinburgh after Flodden":

> *"All night long the northern streamers*
> *Shot across the trembling sky:*
> *Fearful lights that never beckon*
> *Save when kings or heroes die."*

The General himself was the least concerned of all. A young teacher who sat by him one night looked often at the quiet face on the pillow. He wrote: "Never was more beautifully displayed how a long and severe education of mind and character enables the soul to pass with equal step through this supreme ordeal; never did the habits and qualities of a lifetime, solemnly gathered into a few last sad hours, more grandly maintain themselves amid the gloom and shadow of approaching death. . . . As the old hero lay in the darkened room, or with the lamp and hearth fire casting shadows upon his calm, noble front, all the massive grandeur of his form, and face, and brow remained; and death seemed to lose its terrors, and to borrow a grace and dignity in sublime keeping with the life that was ebbing away."

On the 10th of October he seemed better; the 11th found him wandering in mind. He muttered to himself words that none could understand, but once he said in tones as clear as the orders of the battlefield, "Tell Hill he *must* come up." As the day closed, his condition was worse. Although he did not stir often, he continued to babble. The doctors had to admit they could do no more: he was dying. Mrs. Lee was told this and, on her insistence, was wheeled into the room to take her place once again by the side of the man for whom she had prayed through the black vigils of two wars. Silently, hour after hour, she sat there with his moist hand in hers.

The long night ended. Across the campus students began to stir. Presently they straggled to chapel. In the sick room there was silence, the painful breathing of the General, the unintelligible mutter of a mind that was ranging far. Nine o'clock came and passed; the slow hand crept to the quarter; still he breathed. Half after nine, a vague movement, and then the last order before the march: "Strike the tent."

INDEX

Index

#17⁹ᵗ 1342